Decision Accounting

Decision Accounting

Using Accounting for Managerial Decision-Making

Gordon Fraser

Basil Blackwell

HF
5 657.4
.F73
1991
157041
Sept. 1992

First published 1990
First published in USA 1991

Basil Blackwell Ltd
108 Cowley Road, Oxford, OX4 1JF, UK

Basil Blackwell, Inc.
3 Cambridge Center
Cambridge, Massachusetts 02142, USA

British Library Cataloguing in Publication Data
A CIP catalogue record for this book is available from the British Library.

Library of Congress Cataloging in Publication Data
Fraser, Gordon.
Decision accounting: using accounting for managerial
decision-making/Gordon Fraser.
p.   cm.
ISBN 0-631-17309-9
1. Managerial accounting.   2. Decision-making.   I. Title.
HF5657.4.F73   1991
658.15'11—dc20
90-36584 CIP

Typeset in 10 on 12 pt Sabon
by Wyvern Typesetting Ltd
Printed in Great Britain by T J Press Ltd., Padstow, Cornwall.

Contents

viii Contents

1

Introduction

This book is aimed at the business manager who is required to take on a wide-ranging business management role. Part of that role will be to manage the finance and control functions of a separate business, or perhaps a unit of some larger firm. To make the transition from technician to manager it is necessary to have a reasonable grounding in the concepts of financial control. Detailed knowledge is less important, as professional accountants should be relied upon to make the concepts come alive.

Providing accounting systems are used sensibly and within their limitations, they provide a well-proven basis for the successful management of a business. Accounting systems certainly cannot answer all the questions, and if used incorrectly they can be positively misleading. So business managers need to understand accounting jargon and have sufficient grip of the concepts in order to tailor the accounting control systems to suit the way they want to manage the business.

No two companies are identical, whether they are both airlines or electricity utilities or building contractors. The differences are not only operational but also a reflection of the management style of the chief executive. Although accounting systems appear to be governed by immutable laws and rules, these rules can be bent in many different ways to match the peculiarities of the business. This tailoring of accounting and control systems to match the organizational culture is essential if the systems are to be effective.

This book may also be useful to experienced accountants who have hitherto specialized in taxation or financial accounting and now wish to broaden their management accounting experience in preparation for more senior roles.

The book is interspersed with executive comments. These are intended to provide reference points for non-accountants as they may be able to recognize in the executive comments some of the problems that they already face. The executive comments are written from the perspective of a chief executive of a large departmentalized corporation, and some of them may strike a chord with the reader having, as a line manager or financial controller, to respond to the chief executive's needs.

Apart from cash flow, in accounting there is no absolute truth, despite the layman's perception that accountants are accurate human beings. As in religious matters, there are numerous versions of the truth, depending on the concepts to which one subscribes. This book obviously contains the author's version of the truth but it must be recognized that other views exist and some of them have a semblance of merit.

The only way to decide on the truth in accounting is to look at the logic of the individual business situation and see if the accounting information or concept makes sense when stripped of jargon and historical conventions. The reader who is looking for definitive answers in this book will be disappointed. Definitive answers are applicable only to techniques and there are many good text books that explain techniques. This book is primarily concerned with concepts, on the premise that once the concepts are understood, then the techniques become self-evident.

Management reporting systems, if they are to justify their cost, must aid the making of decisions. Business decisions are inevitably complex and hardly ever can there be an objective yes or no answer based on accounting results. Accounting results are just part, albeit an important part, of the myriad of pieces of information, both objective and subjective, that go towards making a decision. That does not mean that there can be any laxity in the provision of accounting information – the businessmen and women must expect the best service possible from their accountants. What it means is that attempts to quantify the unquantifiable must be resisted. Once the pure accounting results become tainted with guesses or flights of fancy, then the decision process is degraded rather than enhanced.

This book addresses six major issues:

Funding and Liquidity Even profitable businesses may suffer liquidity (cash shortage) problems if:

- they are investing more in capital than the normal profits can provide;

- debts fall due for payment and have not been replaced by new lines of credit;
- the bookkeeping systems are inadequate and unexpected liabilities arise at short notice; or
- the business is volatile and there are insufficient cash reserves to meet sudden downturns in trading.

Cash flow is the ultimate truth for any business and must receive the highest priority. Regular and realistic cash flow forecasts are essential and must indicate the future cash position, at least over the next month. Possible cash shortages have to be covered by confirmed credit facilities, even if they never have to be used. The funding for a business can come from a variety of sources and these are explained.

Profitability The concept of profitability is the foundation of decisions by investors and business managers. Profit is looked at from the perspective of the investor, which calls into question the relevance of the statutory accounts that are issued to investors.

A firm must try to reflect the realities of the stock market in the way it manages its business, for if the investors are kept satisfied then the business is at least serving its primary purpose. This requires the business to measure its operating units in terms of their return on capital employed. However, this measure is only an approximation of the investor's measure, which is the growth in the stock price.

Capital Investment Continuing capital investment is needed to sustain long-term growth. Capital investment has to have a payback, although the benefits often cannot be quantified. The allocation of cash to programmes and projects needs to be managed so that it:

- fits within a coherent business strategy;
- does not starve fast-growing business segments because of problems in stagnant segments;
- requires consideration of the various options available to achieve the same result and financial analysis to help choose the best option;
- requires assessment of business risks and an action plan to minimize or control the risks.

Once a project is under way, there has to be tight control over expenditure, timing and quality of output by means of a project control system.

Costing for Pricing Generally, pricing is driven by the external market, but the company may have pricing procedures that give it a disadvantage compared to competitors. The pricing and costing procedures constantly need to be updated and managed so that:

- absorption costing techniques are avoided in case they distort perceptions of cost and consequently distort pricing;
- there is sufficient flexibility in the pricing procedures to allow local competition to be matched;
- pricing is reviewed primarily in terms of market conditions rather than internal cost considerations;
- cost increases are passed on in the form of higher prices only where competitors are likely to be suffering similar cost increases.

Marketing and pricing tactics should be based on a segmentation of the market and a knowledge of whether cross-subsidization is occurring. Segmentation should be evident in the routine contribution reports that are provided to marketing and product design specialists.

Organizational Control A well-founded management reporting system based on financial results is a good indicator that the routine aspects of the business are under control. The signs of a good management reporting system are that:

- the results are reviewed and questioned by senior executives and they follow up on matters raised in previous reports;
- the reporting system reflects, as much as possible, the activities controllable by a specific manager;
- the reports use profitability as a primary focus wherever possible;
- there is some benchmark for comparative performance, either historical results or a budget;
- statistical measures are integrated with financial results to emphasize outputs or achievements rather than pure costs;
- the reports are as frequent as is necessary in the nature of the business, and are prompt and within reasonable degrees of accuracy;
- there is executive comment that demonstrates that line managers understand the financial implications of their actions.

The design of the management reporting system has to consider the vexed question of transfer pricing. The budgeting system needs critical review; too often, budgeting is a mere mathematical exercise that lacks any real substance.

Systems Development As a result of topics raised in the previous sections, various procedural matters are discussed. In particular, there is explanation of user computing as a method of obtaining quick results to satisfy management information needs.

A glossary of common accounting terminology is included at the end of the book.

2

Funding and Liquidity

The ultimate reality for any business is its ability to generate cash and to have enough cash available to pay the wages bill and the creditors. This is such a fundamental requirement that it must be accorded the highest priority. Shortages of cash can lead to penalty interest rates, loss of business opportunities and even foreclosure by creditors; liquidation of the business and forced sale of assets will result in major losses to the investors and employees. To ensure adequate liquidity it is necessary to carry spare cash or lines of credit, and these have a cost in terms either of interest foregone or of fees from the bank for issuing standby credit facilities. Thus there needs to be a balance between safety and the minimization of interest costs and bank fees.

Funding and cash flow management fall into two broad categories. On one hand, there is the need to manage the day-to-day (or hour-to-hour) availability of cash and other liquids, such as debtors and stock. At a total business level, the cash control process needs data from the operating units in the form of cash flow forecasts and details of existing cash balances. This information can then be combined with higher-level considerations such as strategic investments, dividend policy and share issues so that their cash flow impact can be integrated into the day-to-day control process. Having worked out the cash requirements, it is then necessary to manipulate bank accounts and marketable securities to fund cash shortages or to make best use of cash surpluses.

Then, at a higher level, there is the need to organize the financial structure of the business so that there are adequate funds to pursue profitable investment opportunities, and for investments eventually to be realizable into cash that can be used as dividends or for reinvestment. Financial structuring requires decisions on whether to raise debt or seek equity capital. Equity capital funding is a

subjective and emotive area as it gives rise to questions of ownership and control, stock market listings and dividend policy.

Funding and cash flow management are specialist tasks that
should be undertaken by people with knowledge of the underlying
business and with experience of the banking system and money
markets. It is definitely one part of the financial control system
that allows no room for the amateur. These two aspects, day-to-
day management and overall financial structure management, will
now be discussed, beginning with a look at the factors influencing
the overall financial structure of a business.

Responsibility for Funding

> Our line managers are unnecessarily worried about investment
> decisions and where the money is going to come from. I tell them
> that they should worry about the business side of the project and let
> the finance director worry about the cash.

The funding for a business and its investments can be obtained
from:

- existing cash reserves;
- additional borrowings, including leasing alternatives;
- cash from new or existing equity investors;
- deferred payments schemes or complicated share swaps or options
  with the vendor of an asset.

A convenient picture of how a business is funded is available in a
source and application of funds statement (funds flow statement).
It is a report that portrays the flow of cash through the business
and provides a link between the *profit and loss account* and the
movement in cash balances. While it is not the type of report that
provokes specific management decisions, it is a very useful
medium for explaining how the business is being funded and how
this relates to the conventional profit measurement.

The funds flow statement in figure 2.1 shows that in the last six
months, the business's mainstream trading activities have
generated $54.3 million in cash. A further $135 million has been
raised through increased debt, stock issues and the sale of assets.
This money has been used to pay taxes and dividends and to
purchase assets for $105 million. The resulting cash surplus of
$69.3 million has been used to build up working capital, such as
stock, debtors and cash balances, or to repay creditors. During the

	Previous 6 months	Next 6 months
Sources of Funds		
Accounting Profit	52.0	65.0
Adjustments for non-cash items		
Depreciation		
Warranty provision		
Self-insurance provision	2.3	2.4
	54.3	67.4
Increase in long-term debt	30.0	
Issue of equity capital	100.0	
Sale of investments and assets	5.0	2.5
Total cash inflows	189.3	69.9
Application of Funds		
Corporate taxes paid		(15.0)
Dividends paid	(10.0)	(34.0)
Repurchase of stock		
Purchase of assets	(105.0)	(25.0)
Purchase of investments	(5.0)	
Total cash outlays	(120.0)	(74.0)
Resultant Change in Working Capital	69.3	(4.1)

Figure 2.1   Funds flow statement for the six months ended 31/12/X9 ($m)

Comment: So far this year, working capital has increased by $69.3 million. New stock issues of $100 million have been used to finance asset purchases of $105 million. Over the next six months, there will be a minor run down in working capital because of final dividend and tax payments. There is adequate working capital to accommodate this decrease.

next six months, there will be a small run down in working capital, by $4.1 million, because of the need to pay taxes and dividends, plus some more asset purchases. The report can give the chief executive comfort that the business's financial experts know what has happened and what is expected to happen. To serve this purpose, it must be kept free of accounting jargon and clearly explain the dynamics of the cash flows.

Funding alternatives have to be divorced from the assessment of the intrinsic value of the investment. If the investment is no good, then no amount of financial engineering is going to remedy the situation. But once there has been a decision that the project has merit, it is the responsibility of the finance experts to come up with a funding package that will allow the project to go ahead. Usually they arrange a general pool of cash or credit facilities that are not tied to any one investment project. But in certain cases they integrate the funding operations with the physical operations, in the form of *project finance*. This approach is mostly used in large investments, such as an oil refinery, airport or mining project, that require extensive amounts of new capital or debt.

For these large projects, numerous providers of finance have to be brought together and there is probably the desire to hedge various risks, such as with exchange rates and commodity prices. Experts in project finance charge high fees for setting up complex funding schemes which may involve syndicates of risk takers; however, the expense is perceived to be worthwhile in that it makes the difference between whether the project can proceed or not.

Raising funds for business expansion is a specialist task best left to the finance director and his or her advisers. The line business managers can then focus their attention on the success of the physical aspects of the business.

Additional funding is essentially a choice of whether to issue equity capital or to assume more debt. These are high-level strategic decisions as issuing more equity capital can dilute the ownership or reduce the market price of the company and so open avenues for a takeover. Likewise, assumption of extra debt can depress the stock price if it is perceived to have significantly reduced the returns that would normally be owned by the equity investors. There is no exact science attached to deciding on the optimum funding arrangements: it all depends on the prevailing market conditions and the investment community's perception of the company and its risks. The biggest single factor affecting funding options will be the ability to raise equity capital through the stock market.

Stock Market Listing

> The most important goal for us over the next three years must be to build up a solid history of profits that will allow us to be quoted on the stock market. Then we can obtain capital to really allow us to expand.

Obviously an investor in a business wants a return on his or her outlay. This return may come partly in the form of dividends, but mostly it will come through appreciation of the value of the business that the investor jointly owns with numerous other investors with similar motivations. The appreciation in the value of the investment can then be realized by selling the stock to another investor.

The ability actively to trade stocks and shares is vital to the investor and this is where the stock market plays an essential role. The advantage of a stock that is tradeable (quoted or listed) on a stock exchange is that there is a ready market for the stock and therefore it is a liquid asset. The investor may have considerable difficulty in selling an unquoted stock and may not then receive a fair market price because there are a limited number of possible buyers. Thus quoting a stock on the stock market can considerably and immediately raise the value of the stock.

Listing on a stock exchange has its price. The rules for disclosure of information are strict, as are the rules governing the trading of stock, in order to prevent abuse of small investors. These rules impose extra responsibilities on the directors of a company and extra fees payable to auditors and professional advisers. But the extra cost is considered worthwhile in terms of the increased tradeable value of the stock, not only from the investors' view, but also for the company, as it allows access to a huge pool of relatively cheap funds.

Investors put their money into the stock market in order to see their investment grow at a rate that will recompense them for their patience and ability to take risk. They do not normally expect to take any active interest in the company and they hire directors to protect their investment. However, once the investor seeks to gain control of a company, then the scenario changes rapidly and the investor is transformed into a business manager. There remains the basic goal of making a return on investment, but the method of extracting that return takes a different form. The owner of control of a company can use the company's cash flow as if it were his or her own and does not need to pander to the needs of any other stockholders. This means that a controlling interest in a company is often worth more than the sum of small parcels of stock that only give ineffectual voting rights at the annual general meeting.

Apart from the tight reporting rules, the other major drawback of having stock listed on the stock exchange is that unwelcome predators are at liberty to buy the stock and eventually win control, which is usually accompanied by changes in personnel at senior levels of the company. The best defence against a predator is to keep the stock price as high as possible by good business performance, or by arranging for large parcels of stock to be held by friendly investors, such as the staff pension fund.

Diversification and Investors

> As part of our diversification strategy, we made a takeover offer for Consolidated Toys at a price that would favour our existing stockholders. As soon as we announced the bid, our stock price fell 10% and eventually the bid failed.

Many companies have sought to diversify the risk in their cash flow and profits by buying into businesses that have a lower risk profile or which react differently to the inevitable business cycles. Almost by definition, therefore, the acquired company is in a different line of business and the new owners lack experience relevant to that line of business. The theory behind diversification is that the investor wants to own a company with stable profits, and that diversification will provide such stability. This theory provides business managers with a suitable avenue for empire building or for avoiding the stockholder criticisms that inevitably come during a low cycle in a cyclical industry.

Diversification as a strategy has often misfired, and the current strategy is to break up the conglomerates and refocus their management on areas where they have special expertise. This is as it should be, not only for better management, but also because investors can diversify their own risk and need no help from business managers. The investor has the opportunity of spreading his or her personal risk by choosing a diverse portfolio of investments: perhaps 33% in government bonds, 33% in high-risk oil explorers and the remainder in blue-chip industrial companies. Investors put money into a company with some clear knowledge of the risk inherent in that company, and the price paid reflects a risk premium particular to the individual company.

Since investors have the ability to conduct their own diversification strategy, it makes little sense for the managers of the company that they partly own to do this job for them, and probably to make mistakes in the process. As a result, when the investment community sees that a company is diversifying into areas in which it lacks expertise, they downgrade their valuation of the company's earnings potential: the stock price falls. The investors have expressed their opinion on the diversification strategy.

Dividend Payouts

> Over the past five years we have adopted a very generous dividend policy. Our dividend payout rate is one of the best in the market, yet our stock price remains in the doldrums.

In theory, investors should not need to be paid dividends. If investors are short of cash, they can sell a parcel of stock whenever they want to and in whatever volume is required. In practice, all large companies pay dividends, and this is probably for four reasons.

The first reason, albeit an irrational one, is that the investors do not believe that the company is progressing well unless it is capable of delivering a dividend. It is an indictment of the information delivered to investors that it is so inadequate as to require backing up by a wasteful exercise in distributing cheques and dividend warrants. Often one sees the odd situation of a company simultaneously announcing a dividend payout and a stock issue to raise more cash. A similar signalling exercise occurs in some countries where stock is split into smaller units, often termed 'bonus shares'. It is difficult to believe that a rational investor can learn anything from a bonus share issue, because it is nothing more than a financial illusion. Since the investors already own the company, merely subdividing the nominal value of the stock serves no practical purpose at all.

A second, more rational cause of dividends is that some investors do need a regular cash income, either to live off or to pay the interest on the borrowings used to finance the purchase of stock. The transaction cost of the dividend is less than the brokerage cost of selling a small parcel of stock. Many companies have dividend reinvestment options which recognize that investors often do not need their dividend.

Another possibility is that the company does not need the cash or cannot earn as much from the cash as the investor can. While it may be considered an indictment of a company that it cannot think of new investment ideas, it is better to give the cash back to the investor than to keep it and not use it properly.

In some countries, taxation aspects have a major influence on dividend policy, particularly where there is an anomaly between the income tax levied on dividends and the taxation of capital gains.

Dividend policy should have only a minor and indirect impact on the price of stock unless there is a major change in dividend policy which acts as a signal of an underlying business change. For example, a company that suddenly declines to pay a dividend is obviously giving out a strong signal that it has a cash crisis.

In the very short term, the physical payment of a normal dividend lowers the price of the stock by the cash value of the dividend. Say a stock unit has a market price today of $5 and is due to pay a $1 dividend tomorrow. Obviously today's price reflects ownership of the stock plus the ability to receive $1 in cash tomorrow. Thus the underlying value of the stock, that is its future earnings potential, is really only $4, and as soon as the dividend is paid the market price will drop to $4. The stock price including the right to receive the dividend is known as the *cum div.* price, and the price without the right to receive the dividend is known as the *ex div.* price.

Dividends are often no more than a token offering to the investor. Nevertheless, they are a fact of corporate life and must be taken into consideration.

Takeovers

> I have run this company successfully for the last ten years and built it up to its current level of profitability. Any takeover bid is going to succeed over my dead body.

When takeovers occur, the successful bid price is often at a considerable premium to the pre-bid market price; perhaps 30% to 100% more. Since a market price cannot be incorrect, the rapid change in price merely reflects a different set of expectations. The bidder for control of a company makes the bid either because it perceives that it can use the company to generate better cash flows than at present, or because it believes that the market is misinformed about the potential for the company and is undervaluing it. Either way, the company must be worth more to the bidder than the current price and so the current price must rise. After a bid has been announced there should then be a period of trading in the stock between existing owners and the bidder. This trading should result in determination of the eventual bid price, or failure of the bid if the current owners have a higher opinion of the company's future than the bidder.

The rules relating to takeovers are exceedingly complex to protect small stockholders from manipulation by larger stockholders. These rules appear to be necessary because small stockholders have to be encouraged to put money into the stock market and they will not do so if they are given a raw deal by the big players. But often the takeover bidding process is complicated by legalistic ploys designed to extract a higher price or to confound the bid altogether.

One of the major factors in most takeovers is the anxiety of the company directors to preserve their privileges, although this is masked behind the pretence of protecting the investor from an inadequate offer price. It is ironic that directors are frequently reluctant to give useful information to investors yet purport to shield investors from an inadequate bid on the basis that only the directors know the true value of the company. In substance, directors and business managers would rather be answerable to a fragmented collection of small investors than to one large investor which knows what it wants and needs in order to justify the takeover premium that has just been paid. This can result in the actual destruction of value by engaging in 'poison pill' investments and/or the assumption of extra debt: the purpose being to make the company far less attractive to a bidder. So much for directors serving the investor!

Management Buyouts

> We spend so much time satisfying stock exchange listing requirements and countering predators, that if we took the company private, we could greatly enhance performance.

The fact that a company is listed on a stock exchange means that many rules of conduct and disclosure have to be followed and much time spent in keeping the stock exchange authorities content. In recent years there has been a trend towards management buyouts (or leveraged buyouts) in which a small group of investors, including senior managers of the company, buy the business from the existing owners. The purchase is mostly financed by high-risk debt, termed 'junk bonds', which, because of the high-risk premium, carry high rates of interest. These buyout schemes are attractive to self-confident business managers who consider they can generate cash flow that will exceed the high interest rates and put the surplus straight into their own pockets. They are encouraged in this belief by financiers who earn large fees for organizing the funding and change of ownership. Time will tell whether many of these buyouts will have eventually to be relisted as public corporations because of the high risks involved in being heavily geared. When this relisting starts to occur there will inevitably be many burnt fingers among those holding the junk bonds.

Management buyouts pose a tricky problem for the investment community in that there must exist a conflict of interest for the purchasers. The encumbent managers will purchase a business only if they think they can add to its existing value. Yet they are not prepared to add that value for the existing stockholders: they will only do it for themselves. Usually the purchase price is subject to an independent valuation; however, information for that valuation is likely to be considerably biased, as the existing managers are its only source.

From the perspective of an existing owner, whether management buyouts are ethically right or wrong does not really matter: it is a fact of life that a business cannot generate value in a competitive environment without a team of motivated managers. Once the managers decide to make a buyout and assemble the required funds, the process has a momentum that is difficult to stop.

Funding by Debt

> Funny thing, debt. When you don't need the money everybody wants to lend you money, and when you do need the money, they won't let you have it.

Debt as a source of funds is far simpler to understand and manage than equity capital. The lender wants a market rate of interest and certainty of recovering the debt, or a risk premium if there is no certainty of recovery. Stockholders like debt, but only to a certain extent. The reason they like debt is that the net cost after tax is usually less than a company's normal rate of return. For example, if interest rates are 12% and the tax rate is 40%, the net cost of debt after tax is only 7.2%. In an interest rate environment of 12%, companies might be producing, say, a 10% after-tax return on investment. So the investor can borrow money at 7.2% and use it to make 10% returns.

In theory, investors would like the company they own to pile up as much debt as possible because the investors can then make investments without having to outlay their own cash. In practice, there is a limit to the amount of debt a company can assume. The primary constraint is that lenders are unwilling to fund businesses beyond a certain limit, say 50% of the value of the business, although this can vary according to the type of security available. The other constraint is the amount of risk the investor wants to run with against variable interest rates. In a company with a high proportion of debt, cash flow can be severely dented when high interest rates coincide with poor trading conditions, as they often tend to do.

Deciding on the absolute level of debt is an imprecise exercise, with the opportunity for increasing the cash flow attributable to the investor having to be balanced against the constraints. Companies that have a gearing ratio (equity to debt ratio) that is out of line with the norm for similar types of business run the risk of allowing new managers to step in and alter the level of debt to improve the risk profile of the business: once improved, the company is perceived to have a higher value which now belongs to the new owner, not the previous owners. Therefore company directors have to pay close attention to their level of debt if they are to maximize value for existing stockholders.

Raising debt is usually done through banks, which are specialists in assessing the liquidity risk of the companies to which they lend. Banks act as intermediaries between one population of small savers and a different population of borrowers. In providing this service, banks insulate the small saver from the risks attached to specific borrowers. This intermediation service has a cost in terms of the branch network needed to raise the deposits and the inevitable bad debts that go with the risks of lending. Furthermore, the banks have to make a profit on their activities and recover costly liquidity and capital ratios imposed to protect depositors. These costs mean that large and well-respected companies can often raise debt from other lenders at rates lower than those offered by the banks.

Types of Debt

> All we needed was $100 million for three years at the best interest rate, but now the bankers are trying to baffle me with swap agreements and Eurocurrency loans.

Although debt is a very simple business relationship, the financiers have sophisticated debt to meet every subtle need of the customer. Despite these complications, however, lending money can always be reduced to the matters of interest, risk and taxation. To keep up with the latest products, large companies have developed highly specialized treasury functions. This equips them to shop around for the best price on their financing needs rather than stay with one particular bank.

In essence, the finance industry will provide any permutation of a financial deal provided it is legal and they can make some money out of the transaction. The money they make is in the form of either interest margin or fees. The two are effectively interchangeable: if the interest margin is discounted, the fees go up and vice versa.

Financial institutions take on a credit risk when they lend money, as there is a chance that the borrower may be unable to repay the loan. The charge for the credit risk, which is built into the interest rate, reflects the overall credit rating of the borrower plus any special security attached to the loan, such as a registered mortgage. The banks make their own credit-worthiness assessments and also rely heavily on external ratings agencies such as Moodys.

Apart from the credit risk, the financial institution may also carry other risks that the company is unwilling to take on itself. The most common is interest rate risk: the company wants money at a fixed price although interest rates fluctuate day by day. Most financial institutions are happy to provide fixed-rate funding as they have the ability to hedge the risk by taking fixed-rate deposits. Or, if they cannot cover the risk internally, they will go on to the swaps market and find another institution with the opposite need; the two institutions will then do a mutually agreeable swap of interest rate risks.

Foreign exchange risks are similar in concept to interest rate risks: the foreign exchange rates fluctuate day by day and many businesses want to lock in their future transactions at predetermined rates. The financial institutions have dealing facilities where they can buy and sell foreign exchange at current prices or at future prices. They can then offer these future prices to their clients, plus a small profit margin. Similarly, there are institutions that will manage commodity price risks by buying or selling forward contracts of commodities or shares. A funding package may comprise debt, foreign currency dealings and some hedge against commodity prices. It is not easy to make sense of all the offerings from the financiers as the permutations are endless, and sometimes needlessly complex.

Institutions, particularly banks and stockbrokers, are keen to sell their professional or clerical skills to clients. Professional services are usually in the form of financial advice or the bringing together of syndicates that have a joint interest. Banks sell clerical and data-processing services, such as processing cheques and other transactions. There is often cross-subsidization between the clerical and processing services – which lose money – and the borrowing and lending side of the banking business. Some very large corporations can bypass the financial intermediaries, mostly by having their own banking subsidiary.

The following list contains a brief description of common methods of obtaining funding through debt. The terminology varies from one country to another and even from one bank to another.

Overdraft   An overdraft is a variable-sized loan having a maximum limit. Exceeding this limit means penalty interest rates or dishonoured cheques. Fees are usually charged according to the extent of the overdraft limit amount, and there are high and variable rates of interest on the actual overdraft balance. The loan may be secured against some or all of the company's assets.

Term Loan   A term loan is of a fixed amount of money for a specified period and it can be repayable either gradually or in full at the end of the term. Fixed or variable interest rates may apply and the loan can be secured or unsecured.

Project Finance   Project finance is the name given to loans specially designed to match cash flows and risks attaching to a specific project. The loan is usually secured on the project's future cash flow and may be specially organized to suit joint venture projects. It may entail hedging commodity prices, such as for gold or oil, to ensure volatile prices do not jeopardize the ability to repay the loan and interest.

Leasing   Leasing can be thought of as the renting of an asset from a lessor who continues to own the asset and will resume possession at the end of the rental agreement. It can also be organized so that it is just another way of borrowing money; in substance, the lessee owns the asset through an option to purchase at a set price ('residual value') at the end of the lease. Leasing can have some taxation advantages through the timing of tax relief. The monthly or quarterly lease payments include interest and depreciation of the asset. Usually, the lessee is responsible for maintenance and insurance of the asset. Apart from the taxation advantages, leasing is an expensive form of finance and is often a surrogate for a loan to a company which is a poor credit risk.

Commercial Bill Financing   Financing through commercial bills starts with the borrower issuing a piece of paper – 'the bill'. The bill is a promise to pay a set amount of money at a future date including an interest component. For a fee, a bank usually accepts or endorses the bill to guarantee the credit risk: the piece of paper then has a higher value as it has less risk attached to it. A bank or some other lender pays cash for the bill ('discounts it') and so the borrower has obtained the cash required until the bill eventually matures. The person holding the bill can trade it in the money markets and with skilful trading may be able to make a profit if interest rates move. At maturity, the borrower pays the value of the bill plus interest to whoever holds the bill at that date. The interest rates on bills are usually slightly lower than overdraft rates. A *promissory note* is similar to a commercial bill except that it is not usually accepted – guaranteed – by a bank. The purchase of commercial bills is a convenient way for a company to earn interest on its spare cash: the bill can always be sold through a broker if the cash is needed again in a hurry.

Debt Factoring   A business can sell its debtors to a factoring company and so receive cash immediately instead of waiting for customers to pay. Any bad debts are charged back to the company that sold the debt. High interest rates apply, partly to recompense for the extra administrative work involved, making it an expensive form of funding.

Debentures (Loan Stock)   Debentures are long-term loans raised from the public at fixed interest rates. They are usually secured by a charge (mortgage) on the company assets and this is enshrined in a debenture trust deed. The interest rates are lower than those charged by the banks but there is considerable cost in handling numerous small applications. Convertible loan stock is the same as debentures but allows the lender to convert the loan to shares at some date in the future.

A company with spare cash can invest it in commercial bills or in a bank with *at-call deposits* or *term deposits*. At-call deposits can be withdrawn at any time, but low or zero interest rates apply and fees are charged for each transaction. Term deposits can be withdrawn at the end of a specified term and high interest rates apply, but there are penalties for early withdrawal.

The basic financial products are just the starting point for a whole range of subtleties and permutations which give a company almost unlimited scope in the arrangement of its funding. But any funding scheme is inexorably driven by a company's risk profile, as perceived by the bankers, and market-driven interest rates.

Cash Flow Co-ordination

Finance has become such a complex issue that we need dedicated specialists to handle the bankers on level terms and co-ordinate cash flow throughout the group.

The fundamentals of cash flow management are knowing exactly what cash or credit facilities are available and having a reasonable estimate of cash to be received or paid over the next month or two. In a company with numerous business units, cash flow needs to be managed at two levels. At the top level there needs to be a treasury unit to allow specialization of skills, to co-ordinate natural cash flow set-offs between operating units and to provide economies of scale when dealing with bankers and the money markets.

It is not usually feasible, or organizationally desirable, for a central treasury unit to become involved in the day-to-day control of working capital in the business units. So, at a lower level of control, optimization of local cash flow has to be managed by the individual business units through tight control of debtors, work in progress and inventories. The motivation for optimizing cash flow in the business units should exist through the management reporting system, whereby profit is measured as a percentage of capital employed, including working capital. Alternatively, the business units can be charged notional or actual interest on the capital they consume.

Having a small number of good-quality treasury operators in group headquarters can earn or save a great amount in interest. The financial markets are complex, there being a huge number of variations on the basic financial products. Keeping abreast of all the products, knowing good value when it occurs and being able to wrangle the best deal from the financial services industry is a specialist task. Conversely, treasury operators who venture into markets that they do not fully understand, such as foreign exchange futures, can incur enormous losses. Therefore, although it is worth having top-quality treasury operators, they have to be fully accountable and measurable on their activities and they must work within predefined trading limits.

Within a diverse group of business units there are bound to be natural set-offs, that is situations where the cash flow pattern of one business unit counteracts that of another. These set-offs have to be consolidated so that the group is not fragmenting its dealings with the financial institutions. Similarly with foreign exchange, if each business unit were to deal separately with the external financial market, total financial costs would increase in that opportunities would be lost to use any natural set-offs that might arise in the need for foreign exchange. The effect of a fragmented cash management approach is demonstrated in the following example.

The bank may have a 6% spread between how much interest it charges on an overdraft and the rate it will pay for short-term cash deposits. The whole group may need to carry $10 million in cash on average, and at 10% this will cost $1 million p.a. However, at any point in time there may be $150 million in short-term deposit accounts in various business units earning only 4% and there may be $160 million in short-term overdrafts costing 10%. So the real cost is $9 million p.a. (based on $150 million at a 6% cost differential). Thus a net $10 million cash requirement is costing an effective 90% interest rate.

While this may be an exaggeration, it demonstrates the cost of not using natural set-offs, which in this case could have been accomplished by employing one centrally managed cheque account throughout the group, or a series of accounts linked together as part of an agreement with the bank.

As with any piece of business, the bigger the parcel, the better the deal that should be able to be struck. This especially applies in the finance industry, where the clerical cost of a $1 million loan is identical to that of a $100 million loan. Furthermore, the finance industry likes to deal in large-value transactions as these are seen to be prestigious, and this is a further inducement for them to shave the fees and interest rates. Only by bundling up the needs of all the business units is it possible to maximize the economies of scale available in the financial markets, and this can be achieved only with a central treasury unit.

Short-term Cash Management

> Cash flow management entailed the financial controller's typist telephoning the bank each day to ask how much was in the account. This worked fine until she went on holiday: nobody phoned and the bank dishonoured the wages cheque. I am now looking for a new financial controller.

The purpose of the cash flow management system is to ensure that there is sufficient cash to meet liabilities as they fall due while minimizing the amount of cash left idle in accounts that do not pay interest. Some float or contingency cash is inevitable, and its magnitude will be determined by the predictability of the company's cash flows.

A routine control system is essential and it must be derived from the normal accounting records, producing a weekly or monthly cash flow forecast. The example in figure 2.2 shows a cash flow forecast that looks ahead five weeks. From this report it is evident that there may be a minor problem in the fourth week but, as the report comments, this can be overcome by delaying payments to creditors.

The frequency of performing the cash flow forecast depends on the predictability of cash flows. In some businesses a monthly forecast may be sufficient; in others, rolling weekly forecasts are needed, each time adding a new week to the forecast. The level of accuracy concerns not only the amounts, but also their timing. The source data have to come direct from the underlying bookkeeping records and are then combined with some manual intervention. The major sources of information are:

Payroll Data The payroll is one of the most predictable cash flows. The information should be easily estimated from historical trends amended slightly for seasonal bonuses or overtime. Employee deductions and labour-related taxes are normally paid out monthly at set times of the month.

	Week 1	Week 2	Week 3	Week 4	Week 5
Cash Receipts					
Cash from debtors	100	85	120	120	190
Debt issues					
Tax refund				97	
Sale of assets	15				
Cash inflow	115	85	120	217	190
Cash Payments					
Payments to creditors	28	22	158	70	10
Salaries and wages	25	26	25	27	24
Employee taxes			13		
Sales taxes				25	
Purchase of assets					90
Debt repayment		110			
Interest payments			16		
Cash outlay	53	158	212	122	124
Net cash movement	62	(73)	(92)	95	66
Cash and credit available	100	162	89	(3)	92

Figure 2.2   Cash flow forecast for the five weeks to 23/9/X7 ($000)

Note: As a result of this forecast, payment to creditors in week 4 will be delayed slightly to allow a cash safety margin.

Creditors (Accounts Payable) Data   There are worthwhile benefits to be obtained from a modern automated creditors ledger. A modern system should be capable of recording a due payment date for each invoice processed and this then allows routine reports to be produced that show all recorded liabilities and the timing of future cash outlays. This not only allows accurate prediction of payments but also ensures payment at the due date, thereby avoiding interest penalties while retaining cash resources until the last minute.

Frequently, creditors' invoices spend days or weeks 'in the system' while someone marries them to a purchase requisition and goods-received voucher, then approves the invoice. This delay seriously hinders the usefulness of the creditors ledger as a tool for cash fore-casting, as most of the invoices are due for payment almost as soon as they enter the creditors ledger system. There is no commercial gain in being slow to process creditors' invoices, and it frequently causes inefficiency by having to follow up complaints from suppliers. If there is to be an attempt to squeeze an extra credit period from the supplier, then it should be managed properly, not by default through inefficient processing of invoices.

Debtors (Accounts Receivable) Ledger   The debtors ledger provides the main source for predicting cash receipts. In most debtors ledgers, the date of each invoice is recorded, and therefore it should be possible to obtain an analysis of debtors by the age of the invoice. It is unlikely that all debtors will pay on the due date, and there needs to be some empirical analysis of the likely delays. In some businesses there are a small number of customers, in which case there needs to be a customer-by-customer analysis of their history in paying accounts on schedule.

Trade Bills   Some businesses use trade bills, particularly for imports and exports, with the bill maturing once the goods have been landed. The details of these bills should be available in a register which can be used to predict cash flows with a fair degree of accuracy.

Project Managers   Where a business is involved in major projects, the cash flow can depend on architects' certificates or the like. The amount and timing of these certificates is only really known by the project manager or project accountant, who should be required to submit detailed project cash flow forecasts.

It is worth reiterating that cash is the only ultimate truth in business: no cash, no business. Whatever trendy theories may be applied to other facets of managing the business, make sure the cash control system is sensible, proven and reliable.

3

Profitability

The concept of profit only has meaning when it is used in comparison to the investment needed to create that profit: absolute measures of profit are useless in isolation. This comparison of profit to investment is termed *profitability* and it is fundamental to any objective analysis of business success. While the measurement process appears simple, it is fraught with difficulty because the techniques for measurement of both profit and investment are imprecise and variable depending upon the perspective from which profitability is being viewed.

Profitability has to be considered from two perspectives – that of the external investor and that of the manager within the business. While they should both be motivated towards maximizing the profitability of the company, they use different levels of information and different methods of assessing profitability. The external investor has the published accounts, which are of little practical use, and various rumours and half-truths that can be compared against the stock market price, which is an absolute truth in measuring the value of the business.

The business manager has much more detailed information about the source of profits and their future trends, but only an approximate guide to the value of the investment portfolio that he manages. Both perspectives of profitability are flawed to some extent, and outmoded accounting concepts that are used in the published accounts do not help the situation. Since profitability is so fundamental to the business process, it is worth examining how it is measured and how the measurement can be used within a business.

The Profit Concept

> We have put in a lot of hard work over the last two years building an infrastructure for the future. The company is worth a lot more now than it was then, but that does not show up in the accounts.

While anybody can understand cash flow, profit is a much harder concept rationally to explain. Profit is an attempt to compare, in money terms, the difference between resources used and the value passed on to the customer. In practical terms though, profit measurement is limited in that many business functions cannot be measured in money terms. For example, the main asset of a company could be its highly skilled workforce that it has spent years developing and training. If half of them resign, the only entry in the books would be the cost of paying out their pension fund entitlements and the cost of advertising for replacement staff. The effect of the resignations on traditional profit would flow through eventually, although it would never be separately itemized as a cost.

Theoretically it would be possible to estimate the value of all the company's assets, including the value of its skilled workforce, and to see whether that value had increased or decreased. Whether the change in value is called profit or some other term is unimportant – at least it might be possible to say whether a business contains more value today than it did one year ago. A change towards this style of accounting is most unlikely as it makes the measurement system too subjective for the comfort of auditors and regulators. Therefore profit is restricted to being a refinement of cash flow and the difference between them needs to be explained.

The difference between cash flow and profit is most marked in businesses that are either growing rapidly or at a very mature stage. Consider a property development company in two different phases of its evolution. Initially it invests heavily in new sites and has a large cash outflow but minimal profits or losses. Later it sells the properties and reports a profit, as shown in figure 3.1. At the end of the buying and selling process the cash flow and profit are the same, but in both the first and the second accounting periods there are huge divergences between cash flow and profit.

So far as assessing the success of the business is concerned, the profit and loss account gives a more correct view of the company's operations: that is, the business did not lose $17.5 million in the

	Year 1	Year 2	Year 1 + 2
Cash Flow			
Purchase site	(5.0)		(5.0)
Sale proceeds		26.0	26.0
Development costs	(10.0)	(2.0)	(12.0)
Administration costs	(1.0)	(1.0)	(2.0)
Interest paid	(1.5)	(1.0)	(2.5)
Cash Flow	(17.5)	22.0	4.5
Profit and Loss Account			
Sales income	0.0	26.0	26.0
Cost of sales	0.0	(19.5)	(19.5)
Trading profit	0.0	6.5	6.5
Administration costs	(1.0)	(1.0)	(2.0)
Profit Before Tax	(1.0)	5.5	4.5

Figure 3.1   Profit and cash flow difference: building developer ($m)

Note: In this example the company includes interest as a cost of sales. Other companies
may write off the interest as it is incurred.

first period and did not make profits of $22 million in the second period.

The following examples demonstrate the divergence between cash flow and profit and loss:

Purchase of a Fixed Asset   The cash flow occurs at the time of purchase. The profit and loss account ignores the capital outlay but each month for the next, say, five years there is a depreciation charge, until the asset is 'written off'.

Purchase of Stock for Resale   The cash flow occurs at the time of payment for the goods. The profit and loss account ignores the payment but recognizes the cost each time part of that stock is eventually sold to a customer, when it is compared to the sales proceeds and the profit is reported.

Sale of Goods on Credit The cash flow does not occur until the customer pays. The profit and loss account recognizes the income when the goods are delivered to the customer.

These divergences between profit measurement and cash flow measurement are all timing differences, which means that the cash flow report and the profit and loss account will eventually give the same answer, at some infinitely distant time in the future. Until that time, the cash flow report and the profit and loss account will report different values.

Profit Measurement

We pay a fortune for accountants and auditors to make sure our published accounts are totally correct. This seems to be spurious accuracy as we are required to make huge assumptions about the value of our inventories and investments.

Conventional accounting is termed *accrual accounting* because it is based upon the concept of matching income and costs to the time at which value is created or destroyed. To achieve this, accrual entries are passed through the ledger according to a set of ever more complex rules. These rules, known as *accounting standards*, are constantly being refined in the belief that there is some absolute level of truth that can be presented in the accounts. This search for the correct answer has taken a tortuous trail as accountants have tried to make changes amid great apathy from the businessmen and women and investors who are the supposed users of the statutory accounts.

The problem with accounting standards is that the underlying format of statutory accounts was laid down in the nineteenth century when business was a great deal simpler than it is now. Many of the modern sophisticated business deals and relationships cannot be translated into a set of nineteenth-century accrual accounts without the use of gross simplifications or excessive rules that create anomalies and loopholes. Accounting standards keep plenty of people busy designing, explaining, modifying and interpreting the rules, but conventional accounting concepts are inevitably limited in portraying the health of a business.

The apathy from the business community towards any worthwhile change stems from the fact that business managers do not want to tell their competitors anything that would be useful to them. Nor do business managers want to give investors any leverage to ask informed questions about the performance of the company. In both regards the hieroglyphics that pass for the statutory accounts meet the managers' requirements. If the investors are to be told anything, it will be what the business managers want them to know and not what the accountants think they ought to know.

The apathy from the investors comes from the fact that they are happy with the inside knowledge, rumour and selective information that they already receive. Perhaps the investment community does not believe that it is possible to deliver any information to them that is better than what they already receive. If this is the case, then it is up to the accounting profession to persuade them that something better can be done.

The statutory accounts, as a source of information on which decisions can be based, are severely limited. Their main role is in that ill-defined area of 'accountability', which was the original intention of the company accounts when they were designed a hundred years ago. To some extent, the publication of a set of accounts and the annual audit is a deterrent against wholesale abuse of the investors' money by the business managers. But the cost in terms of auditing fees and corporate compliance with accounting standards runs into many millions of dollars each year for any large business.

Despite the profusion of accounting standards and an extensive and skilled accounting profession, the determination of profit is highly subjective. It must be so because there is still no clear definition of what a set of published accounts is supposed to achieve, and without that definition it is not possible to manage the process to deliver a worthwhile product. For example, the profit and loss account is the difference between two balance sheets, and is eternally damned because nobody really knows what a balance sheet is supposed to demonstrate: it is not a statement of 'value', nor is it a valuation of a business.

The standard defence is that, 'while the statutory accounts may be nonsense, at least it is consistent nonsense and so provides a benchmark for comparative performance measurement'. Frequently the benchmark is shifted, either by use of some loophole in the accounting standards or by the regulators changing the standards. Then only the most skilful and diligent financial expert can unravel the tangle to discern the effect of the change.

But not even the 'consistent nonsense' defence is a satisfactory argument for continually fine-tuning an outmoded nineteenth-century accounting concept.

Profit Expectations

When investing, the only thing that matters is the future, so I don't see how a set of accounts that contains historical information is of any use to the investor.

Investors receive the standard set of accrual accounts, yet any significant movement in share price is usually independent of the release of those accounts. So the investor must be receiving additional signals which are indicators of the performance of the company. These signals take the form of information supplied by research analysts in the stockbroking firms, newspaper articles and information released by the company either deliberately or inadvertently. These signals form an incomplete jigsaw of information that goes to serve one purpose, that of valuing the future health of the business.

Historical information is of use only if it gives some indicators of the future. For some firms that are solely in one line of a mature business, it may be possible to project future profits based on past performance. In most cases, the profit trend will serve only to indicate that the firm's management team has a track record of success, and this can be used to infer that the success will continue.

The relevance, or rather the irrelevance, of historical profits is demonstrated in the price–earnings ratios that are published for quoted stocks. This ratio compares the current market price of a share with the last issued profit result. It can be assumed that the stock market is a perfect market without major distortions, although this is not always a safe assumption when insider trading occurs. Since it is a perfect market, the returns required by all investors are very similar. So they price the stock according to the return they expect to achieve from it. If investors want a 10% return, and if they believe that profit reflects the increase in value of their investment, they will value a company at ten times its level of profit.

This does not happen: a review of the price–earnings ratios reveals a wide disparity. At the extreme, some stocks trade at a ratio of 5:1 while others trade at 50:1 in the same market on the same day. This disparity demonstrates that investors are valuing the stock on a basis other than historical profits. In fact, the valuation can only be based on expectations of future profits. Investors need some form of profit statement from the firm upon which they can base their expectations, but the spurious accuracy of the statutory accounts is irrelevant when its content is only used as part of a broad assessment of future profits.

Profitability Targets

> The board measures me on the stock price and I have to make sure that I evaluate the operating divisions on a similar basis.

The ultimate measure of success for a business is the growth in its stock price, which in turn is influenced by its future earnings capacity. The stock price is set by the stock market and, while it is a broad reflection of the performance of the company, it is remote from the performance of individual operating units within the company. The general principles that apply to movements in the stock price, the returns on amounts invested, can be approximately applied to the internal measurement of operating units. Therefore the operating units can be measured on how much capital they consume and the profits that come from using that capital. This key measure, known as *return on capital employed*, can flow down through the business in one form or another. To set up this measurement system, it is necessary to define 'return' and what is meant by 'capital employed'.

Return, in this context, means profit. Profits, as usually defined to the outside world, are calculated after interest and taxation has been deducted from the operating income. But when evaluating operating units within a business, it is best to measure profits before interest and taxation charges. By using profit calculated before interest and tax, all the operating units are placed on a comparable basis because anomalies caused by local debt considerations or taxation idiosyncrasies are removed. Furthermore, within a large departmentalized business, both debt and taxation strategies have to be managed centrally and the operating units should be assessed and managed without the funding and taxation juggling acts that can confuse their reported profits.

In accounting terms, capital employed is the same as the net assets of a business unit. If profit is to be measured before interest costs, then net assets should also be measured by disregarding any external debt held by the business unit. Assets are normally measured as the book value of fixed assets plus working capital. This raises the question of how the assets are valued, in particular properties and intangible assets such as goodwill. The historical cost accounting concept records assets at their original purchase price. Thus a factory purchased twenty years ago for $100,000 may still be in the books at that amount, or even lower, if it has been depreciated; yet its current value may be $1 million. The company has the opportunity to release that value for the shareholders by selling the property and, if necessary, leasing it back again. It is unrealistic to compare profits against a $100,000 investment when the real investment is $1 million. Therefore, capital employed should reflect the current value of the assets.

When a business changes hands, the purchaser usually pays a premium over the book value of the assets. This premium, known as *goodwill*, reflects two components:

- the difference between the real market worth of the assets and the traditional method of recording assets at historical cost, which ignores the value of intangible assets such as patents, trademarks, brand names and customer loyalty;
- an expectation of being able to improve the future value of the business by better management, economies of scale or financial restructuring.

Although a business creates intangible assets as it progresses, these are not usually valued until the business unit is sold. Theoretically, goodwill should be periodically valued and included in the calculation of capital employed, so reflecting the opportunity cost of retaining the assets. In practice this is not done because it introduces too much subjectivity into the calculation process. As a result, return on capital employed is not strictly comparable to the opportunity cost to the investor of owning the business. For example, the accountants may define capital employed as $10 million, while the market value of the company might be $20 million. Since the investors have the opportunity to sell the company for $20 million, they must evaluate their returns against that opportunity. But within the business, the business manager can evaluate returns only against the asset values, which are said to be $10 million. Thus there is a discontinuity between the investor's calculation of returns and that of the business manager.

Despite these limitations to translating stock market realities into the day-to-day life of the company, return on capital employed is the nearest approximation that can be used within the confines of conventional accounting.

Having set specific targets for return on capital employed, it then remains to adjust the targets to reflect local circumstances. For instance, a newly formed business segment is unlikely initially to meet group-wide targets. Likewise star performers in the group will have to perform well ahead of the group average in order to make up for the newly emerging businesses.

The example in figure 3.2 shows how the return on capital employed is used to create targets for profitability for individual parts of the business. The company in this example is making a 12% return for its investors at present, as measured by a net profit after tax of $280 million on a market value of the equity of $2,300

Group Balance Sheet		Profit and Loss Account	
Assets	2,200		
		Operating profit	520
		Less:Interest	(120)
Equity	1,000		
(Market value $2,300)			400
Debt	1,200	Less: Tax	(120)
	2,200	Net profit	280

Stockholders' Return		
Net profit	280 =	12%
Market value of stock	2,300	

Return on Capital Employed		
Operating profit	520 =	24%
Assets	2,200	

Divisional Performance	Total	Coal	Oil & Gas	Air Freight
Assets	2,200	1,000	1,000	200
Operating profit	520	180	320	20
Return on Capital Employed	24%	18%	32%	10%

Figure 3.2   Coal, Oil & Gas Shippers Group: financial results ($m)

million (the $2,300 million market value compares to the historical investment of $1,000 million).

Disregarding interest costs and taxation, the company is making a 24% return, as measured by $520 million of profit compared to assets of $2,200 million. This rate of return has significantly affected the market value of the stock and forms a relative benchmark for future performance (and historical trend analysis), and one that can be used within the company, based on its normal accounting systems. The assets for each operating division and their operating profits are listed to show the return on capital employed from each of the operating units. In this instance, the Oil & Gas Division is the star performer, Coal is dragging down the group total and Air Freight is a new business yet to make adequate returns. Armed with this information, the chief executive is able to make some broad targets for future performance. A return of at least 24% must continue to be made, otherwise the stock price is likely to decline. It is useless to set a blanket 24% target, which Coal and Air Freight are unlikely to achieve. Nor can Oil & Gas be allowed to reduce significantly its returns, as it is propping up the rest of the group. In practice, the chief executive might say:

Coal: I know there is a downturn in the industry at present. However, I want you to aim for improvement to a 20% return on capital employed this year, with an improvement to 24% within the next three years.

Oil & Gas: Last year was exceptional but we cannot afford for your returns to drop below 30% next year.

Air Freight: This is a growing market where good rates of return are expected. Your target is 20% return on capital employed for next year.

Each of the operating divisions, having been given these targets, can in turn go through their individual activities to decide how to achieve the desired result.

Return on Capital Employed is a fundamental ratio that equates the value created (profit) to the assets used for the purpose. It has a similarity to the expectations of the stockholders and as such it projects some of the stock market realities into the day-to-day life of the business.

4

Project Appraisal

Business investment is obviously motivated by the expectation that cash returns will outweigh the original outlay. Therefore financial evaluation, whether strict or informal, is essential. The difficulty lies in making a direct connection between the initial outlays and the eventual payback. Sometimes the payback is easily visualized, but often many estimates and assumptions are required to help decide whether the investment is worthwhile. This chapter looks at the methods of assembling financial estimates so that they can be sensibly used to assist the investment decision process.

The reasons why businesses invest can be broadly categorized as follows:

Stay in Business This is where the need to invest is imposed by regulation (such as pollution control), competitors (such as the need to respond to a technical breakthrough) or the consumers (who demand a safer or more reliable product). Since such investments are imposed on the business, the investment appraisal system has to focus not on whether to do it, but on which is the best way to do it.

Productivity This is the need to reduce the cost of operations and so improve profits. An investment strategy cannot ignore the fact that in the future, as in the past, costs and prices will fall in real terms – land being the obvious exception. The gradient of this fall in costs depends on the maturity of the product: for example, in real terms, computer costs and prices are probably falling at 30% per annum, whereas motor car costs are probably falling at 5% per annum and bread costs may be falling at only 0.5% per annum. The gradient of the fall in costs, known as the *learning curve effect*, accords with the volume produced by an individual company or by the industry in general. It is one of the reasons why market leadership is important: the business that leads in the market carries with it proportionately more manufacturing volume than its competitors and therefore more experience in cost reduction.

Justification for investment in productivity improvements can often be rigorously evaluated by comparing the expected fall in costs with the outlay needed to achieve the cost reduction. After the event, the fall in costs may be difficult to measure as so many other changes will have occurred that it is impossible to isolate the benefits from any one investment. This does not eliminate the need to quantify and justify the savings that are expected to occur.

Business Expansion   This connotes doing more of the same, either to increase market share or to satisfy growth in demand. Such investments have a sound historical base on which to assess future payback, but the key variable is the prediction of market volume increases and timing of those increases. Subject to inevitable latitude in demand forecasts, the investment should be justifiable in strictly financial terms.

New Products   These are ventures into new fields, some of which are a logical extension of existing operations. An investment strategy has to recognize that products can have a limited life cycle which may vary from months to decades according to the type of market. There has to be a constant investment in the search for replacement products and markets. In this context, new products mean ventures into the unknown, and such ventures carry a far higher risk than merely expanding established lines of business. The risks can be minimized by thorough market research, pilot production plants and recruitment of specialist staff. However, it is unrealistic to expect a financial appraisal to be much more than a financial scenario based largely on hope.

Strategic Investments (e.g. Diversification or Vertical Integration)
These are attempts to reduce reliance on the existing markets or to protect markets or lines of supply. There is certainly the intention of making a satisfactory payback and some financial evaluation is required. However, because of the strategic nature of the project, a long-term view is appropriate. Therefore the financial analysis may focus on the cost impact of the investment, while the benefits might have to be left unquantified.

The success of past business investment decisions is measured to some extent in the financial accounts, where the assets in the balance sheet can be compared to the profits shown in the profit and loss account. It is almost certain that the assets and profits shown in the accounts will be totally different to those in the investment appraisals that spawned those assets and profits. The only thing certain about a financial forecast is that it will be wrong. The skill is in minimizing the error or in not wasting time forecasting factors that defy sensible quantification.

The quality of investment decisions is ultimately set by the level of scrutiny imposed by the executives who approve the projects. They will be experienced enough to identify fuzzy proposals for mainstream activities; however, they may be hoodwinked in some specialist support areas such as premises, transport and computers where they have to rely on the competence of the technical specialists they employ. They should be able to rely on their accountant to impose some quality control on investment proposals, not only in terms of the mathematics but also in seeing that a rigorous and sensible business analysis has been done.

Diversified Investment Portfolios

> The ballbearing industry has been good to us but there is no room for us to grow. I think that gene technology is a growth industry and we should be investing our spare cash in that or some similar business.

Nearly all businesses are diversified to some extent, if only by having a range of products and a range of customers. In a broader context, a diversified firm is one which comprises a number of businesses that may have little in common with each other except that they have the same owner. Diversification as a business strategy has its justification in the proposition that a firm can use the cash flow from one profitable segment (termed a *cash cow*) to finance growth businesses (termed *stars*). This strategy views the firm as a portfolio of investments and naturally there will be some failures that have to be closed or sold if the current owners cannot migrate them into being cash cows.

The theory is that, at an early stage of the business life cycle, the emerging business segment needs a lot of cash to finance its growth and this need for cash cannot be supported out of current profits. Once the industry matures, there will be a strong market leader and a small number of minor competitors. This state will arise through a series of business mergers or bankruptcies as various competitors find they cannot sustain the large drain on cash needed to maintain their market share. When the industry is in a steady state the market leader will be highly profitable as its size and image will confer advantages that competitors will find difficult to counter. This observation of the market seems to make sense when looking at the status of a number of mature industries. It does not mean that it is a vindication of the strategy of firms becoming diversified investment portfolios as it connotes that the owners are performing an investment allocation role that the stock market and banking systems are more efficient at doing.

Diversification as a business strategy is now out of favour with investors as it is seen to lead to dilution of management skills through ventures into fields where the owners have no special ability. Many of the large conglomerates are under pressure to disentangle themselves from their non-core businesses. However, diversification will no doubt continue as a normal part of business because there are inevitably certain industries, such as tobacco, that are withering and their management will always be tempted to look for high-growth alternatives.

The debate about diversification and related management skills is subjective in that definitions of the 'market', and thus of 'market leadership' or 'management skills', are imprecise. Some conglomerates would argue that their business is in manufacturing and this allows them to add value in the production of cars, planes and computers. Likewise other conglomerates profess to being in the financial services business and so they are capable of managing banks, insurance companies and pension fund investments. So far as investment policy is concerned, the major issue is whether, in a diversified firm, some businesses are constrained by the poor performance of the other parts of the investment portfolio.

The theory was that the cash cows in the investment portfolio should be milked to provide cash for the stars of the future. To put this theory into action requires a brave assessment that the cash cow has limited growth potential and that its investment plan should be restricted to that needed to maintain market share. This course of action is likely, at best, to be a self-fulfilling prophecy in that the cash cow is doomed to an unexciting future with restricted opportunity for expansion and a stagnant management team. Most likely, this policy is the precursor to decline and eventual loss of market share to younger and more aggressive competitors. This debate is fought out every day on the stock market through takeover bids for conglomerates and through management buyouts.

If the diversified firm is to act as a portfolio manager, then it has to have the skills not only of valuing and buying potential stars,

but also of valuing and selling *dogs*, the term given to non-per-
forming businesses. Valuation of a business is essentially an investment decision in which the acquisition price has to be compared to
the future cash flows. This topic is covered in more detail
subsequently.

Investment Programming

> We are good at controlling individual projects, yet when we look
> back over the past two or three years it is difficult to see any pattern
> or strategy in why we spent the money.

There are five separate control points in the investment process,
namely:

- setting investment strategies and programmes;
- making decisions on specific investments;
- managing the cash flow to support investments;
- implementing projects; and
- managing the business to realize the payback on the outlay.

This section looks at the organization of a planning process that
integrates the first three functions.

Setting investment strategies is a high-level process that has to
be restricted to a few senior executives. The high-level strategy
evolves continuously and is not something that has to be
integrated closely into the annual budgeting exercise. It is a back-
drop to the annual budget. Specific investments and their operational and cash flow impacts are matters that need to be reflected
in the annual budget.

In the annual budget it is important to recognize the difference
between amounts approved for a project and actual cash flow. The
annual budget has to recognize only the cash flow impact of a
programme or project. There are two reasons for this. Firstly, in
bookkeeping terms, it is only the cash outlays that will be recorded
as actual expenditure. More importantly, if constraints have to be
imposed, they will be as a result of a shortage of cash. A major
part of the annual budgeting process is to identify whether too
much investment cash is being asked for. If cash availability is a
constraint, as it is likely to be, then the budget is the avenue by
which to consider priorities or delay certain programmes.

At any time there will be projects in progress, some that have
been approved but not yet started, some that have not yet been

approved but are likely to occur and others that are unknown but will happen. So when preparing the annual budget, it is possible to be precise about only some of the future investments. If the annual budgeting process forces people to articulate all their projects for next year, there is the danger that the annual budgeting process turns into a forum for approval of individual projects. This is highly undesirable as it arbitrarily compacts many decisions into a few weeks of the year while the budget is being compiled.

Rather than budget for individual projects it is better to budget at a broader level of detail and this can be done by recognizing the difference between *investment programmes* and *investment projects*. An example should serve to clarify the distinction between a programme and a project.

Investment Programme

In order to expand activities in the South East, we intend to spend a maximum of $10 million over the next three years which will encompass a new refrigerated distribution depot and 10,000 square metres of retail shop space.

Investment Project

As part of the South East expansion programme, we have identified a 2 acre site in Southtown suitable for the new depot. We have been offered a twenty-year lease at $200,000 p.a. and it will cost $3 million to build the depot.

Although the Southtown project can be quantified for purposes of the annual budget, there are probably other parts of the South East expansion programme that will occur in the next year and that cannot yet be defined. So the annual budget should be compiled at the programme level. As part of this, someone will have to estimate how much will be spent this year, next year and the year after.

The budget summary in figure 4.1 shows how individual programmes have been summarized and compared to a cash ceiling that has been set after a consideration of profit expectations and dividend and debt strategies. The cash flow has been segregated into priorities so that it provides a ready indicator of what leeway exists to trim cash flow as a result of further consideration of the annual budget.

It has to be decided whether the total company investment is built up from the requests from its business units, or whether it is

	Next year	Next year +1	Next year +2
Projects already committed	0.4		
Stay in Business			
Health regulations	0.5	0.2	
Plant replacement	0.8	0.9	1.2
Strategic Investments			
Northern Canners	1.5		
Business Expansion			
Manufacturing	1.2	1.8	2.0
Distribution	0.3	0.1	0.2
Productivity			
Various projects	0.1	0.6	2.0
New Products			
Various projects	0.0	0.3	2.0
Forecast cash flow	4.8	3.9	7.4
Cash flow limit	5.0		

Figure 4.1   Capital budget summary: cash flow forecast ($m)

an allocation of what the company wishes to spend. In practice, the programmes from the individual business units need to be aggregated and compared to the total feasible. If capital rationing has to occur, then high-level decisions are needed based on growth prospects for the particular business unit and the business unit's potential to exploit those opportunities. Apart from cash constraints, there exists the limitation on management ability to cope with a number of development projects while simultaneously trying to manage day-to-day operations.

Allocation of capital to an investment programme requires some broad assessment of the return possible from that investment. Furthermore, the investment programme has to be viewed as part of a continuing programme that should not be turned off and on year by year. An example of the decision-making process surrounding the forecast shown in figure 4.1 might be:

1 We have a maximum of $5 million that we can invest next year.

2 There is a firm commitment to spend $0.4 million on jobs already in progress or jobs that will soon start.
3 We have stay-in-business requirements of $0.5 million as a result of new health regulations.
4 Our option to purchase Northern Canners will expire in six months. I think this will be a good strategic investment for us as it will allow us to migrate into the health food end of the market. We will probably have to pay $1.5 million to exercise our option on Northern Canners.
5 Our core business is growing at 30% per annum and we need to invest $1.5 million next year just to keep pace with demand.
6 We should spend $0.8 million on replacing worn-out delivery trucks and packing machinery, although we could delay this a bit longer without any serious consequences.
7 That leaves us with $0.3 million that could be spent on new products and productivity improvements. If all the other activities go ahead, I think the management will be too stretched to cope with many other projects and so $0.1 million is a reasonable estimate.

If the budgeting process had required each project to be spelled out precisely, the result would have been much time wasted in trying

	Already spent	To be spent	Forecast total
Stay in Business			
Health regulations	0.35	0.26	0.61
Plant replacement	0.23	0.06	0.29
Strategic Investments			
Northern Canners	0.00	2.10	2.10
Business Expansion			
Manufacturing	0.98	0.21	1.19
Distribution	0.15	0.18	0.33
Productivity			
Various projects	0.08	0.19	0.27
New Products			
Various projects	0.56	1.30	1.86
Cash flow	2.35	4.30	6.65
Cash flow limit			5.00

Figure 4.2 Capital expenditure report: cash flows to June 19X9 ($m)

to quantify preliminary project costs, and the big picture would have been lost in a welter of spurious detail.

Having set the annual budget in this fashion, it is important to report actual results in a similar format. The timing of actual expenditures may be quite unpredictable and so it is useless to compare year-to-date cash flow against a year-to-date budget. The only important factor is whether the annual cash constraint is likely to be exceeded. Thus financial reporting must be a comparison of the latest full-year expectation versus the full-year budget. If this reveals that a budget overrun is to occur, then decisions are required on whether this is permissible or whether some expenditure has to be deferred or cancelled. This approach to reporting is demonstrated in figure 4.2.

Financial Appraisal

> I have been in this business thirty years and I know a good deal when I see one. The financial appraisals are just a double check that my intuition is still working.

As a completely separate exercise to the capital cash flow budgeting, there needs to be a mechanism to appraise individual project proposals to decide whether a project is worthwhile and/or to decide which is the best option for achieving the desired result. For example, new health regulations require that approximately $0.5 million will have to be spent. This is a stay-in-business option (i.e. not an option!) and so there is no need to be involved in any lengthy cost–benefit justification process. However, there are numerous ways of meeting the new health regulations: some are labour intensive with no capital outlays while others require minimal labour but sophisticated cleaning equipment. Deciding on which of these is the best option is an area where detailed financial analysis can be very helpful, if for no other reason than that the analysis process crystallizes many of the vague notions that surround perceptions of the best option.

Even if the financial analysis cannot provide a clear-cut answer on whether the investment is good or bad, at least it may provide some help in clarifying the issues and give a broad view of the costs and possible benefits. There are sound analytical techniques for examining potential projects, but the danger is that these are taught as scientific tools when in fact they are nothing more than a logical presentation of financial estimates. And financial estimates alone are never enough adequately to describe the value of a project. So the financial estimates have to be seen as only a part (sometimes a minor part) of the decision process.

As suggested earlier, the level of rigour used to justify a project depends on the circumstances. Stay-in-business and strategic investments will require justification criteria different from those relevant to productivity programmes or business expansion. So before engaging in any detailed financial analysis, it is worth considering the level of certainty that a businessman or woman can reasonably expect to have before spending investment money.

Businesses are faced with a decision on whether to spend or not to spend. They will make the decision to spend once they have achieved a level of certainty that they will be making the best choice. Once they have achieved that level of certainty, further analysis is irrelevant. Sometimes that certainty can be achieved almost instantaneously: 'I've been in this business for twenty years and I know a good deal when I see one. And this is it.' No further financial analysis is going to change this man's mind. However, he may well need to convince his superiors. Therefore he will have the accountants prepare financial analyses and he will make sure the assumptions they use will give the answer he expects. Unfortunately, much of an accountant's time is spent on such fruitless exercises.

Another businessman may be less certain and say to his accountant, 'This looks like a good proposition so please tell me what the payback will be.' Once he knows the payback period, he may have reached a sufficient level of certainty to make his decision. But he may still be undecided and want more confirmation, so he may ask how the proposal looks when subjected to a discounted cash flow analysis. All the time his certainty is being enhanced until at some point he is confident enough to say yes or no to the proposal.

Theoretically, the approach of gradual appraisal should be sufficient. There should only be as much financial analysis as is needed for confident decision-making. In practice, especially in large bureaucracies, there is the tendency to analyse proposals in extreme detail, even if the analysis is based on biased assumptions, as a personal protection against the possible failure of the project. Thus every possible kind of financial test is used in the belief that these tests demonstrate a rigorous assessment of whether the project is viable. Apart from the waste of effort, the danger is that the culture of the bureaucracy places reliance on the mathematics of extensive financial analyses instead of on the instrinsic soundness of the business proposition. This is a factor that must be borne in mind when trying to design a systematic approach to the approval of investments in large companies.

Project Documentation

Before, we had no formal investment approval process and many inadequate proposals were presented. Now we have a tight set of procedures, but I worry if this has killed some good ideas that might otherwise have surfaced.

Project investment decisions are essentially a choice of options – whether to do it or which one to do – and so the fundamental purpose of an investment appraisal system has to be to encourage the submission of sound options. The chief executive does not have a mortgage on good ideas and has to rely on the imagination and skill of his or her subordinates. The chief executive should not be submerged in a proliferation of proposals, and the investment decision process has to balance the weeding out of inadequate proposals with not inhibiting the flow of ideas.

Within the business there needs to be a constant flow of investment proposals. Some would argue that if an investment proposal meets predetermined guidelines then it should pass easily through the system, and conversely that proposals outside the guidelines should not even be submitted as they waste the time of senior executives. The truth of this argument rests on the shape of the guidelines. If the guidelines are framed in terms of strategic objectives, thorough research and reasonable assumptions, then the guidelines serve a worthwhile purpose. But if the guidelines are merely a mathematical exercise, no matter how complex, without the need to demonstrate the underlying quality of the proposal, then the guidelines are counterproductive: they will favour the bureaucrats at the expense of the entrepreneurs.

The essential requirements of an investment appraisal system are that:

- The project has to be described in business terms and, in particular, each proposal has to relate to an established business strategy: if it does not do so, then the first step is to have the strategies changed. It should not be a case of the tail wagging the dog: strategies cannot be allowed to evolve through piecemeal acceptance of projects.

INVESTMENT PROPOSAL FORM

Date: .... Proposer: ....
Division: ....
Investment programme(s): ....
Proposal title: ....
306Project cost: ....
Description:

Budget availability: $

        Annual programme budget:
        Less: Already committed: (— — —)
        Still available:
        This project, this year: (— — —)
        Remaining after this project:

Net present value:............. IRR: .... Payback: ....
Risk assessment:
  Customer: High / Low / None
  Competitor: High / Low / None
  Technological: High / Low / None

Project priority: Essential / Important / Preferable

Dependencies:

Success Criteria:

Approvals/Support:
Sales .... Date: ....
Production .... Date: ....
Finance.. Date: ....
General management.. Date: ....

Start date: .... End date .... Actual cost: ....
Success achieved? ....
Project manager: .... Date:........

Figure 4.3   Global Publishers investment proposal form

- The proposal must spell out the business risks inherent in the project, how those risks will be managed and whether they have been factored into the financial analyses.
- The impact on cash flow constraints has to be summarized (i.e. can the project be covered by existing budget allowances?).
- There must be a statement of the measure that will be used to monitor the success of the project and a description of the mechanism that will be used to control implementation.
- Dependencies on other activities and projects need to be described: other parts of the organization that are affected by the project must be allowed to comment on the project's impact on their own operations.
- Where relevant, the results of financial evaluation should be presented.

There is a temptation to use standard forms for presentation of investment proposals. In firms large enough to warrant standard forms there is usually such a variety of investment decisions that any one forms design is going to contain a high degree of redundancy. Only where there is much repetition of the investment decisions, for example with equipment replacement, would a standard worksheet be of value. The optimum approach is to have a series of guidelines and one standard summary form. To this would be attached as much detailed supporting information as was thought appropriate. Figure 4.3 demonstrates an investment proposal summary form.

Investment Risks

Every worthwhile investment carries with it some risk. When I see an investment proposal, I want to know what are the risks. I don't expect to be told there are no risks.

Since investment and risk go hand in hand, the method of making investment decisions has to focus heavily on the risks, estimate their impact and see how they can be managed. Experienced operators in an industry develop a keen intuition for the risks in a venture and are able to discount the bullish forecasts in an investment proposal. The experienced operator looks for one or two key indicators in the investment proposal and decides very quickly whether the venture is an acceptable risk.

This intuitive approach to investment, based on hard-won experience, is very important, but it does not mean that an investment proposal should not contain a rigorous risk assessment. The proposer of the investment should be forced to think through all the possibilities, and this will help to define how the project is to be managed, as it will highlight particularly critical areas that will need close control.

Risks can be segregated into two broad categories, namely *business risk* and *financial risk*. The business risks belong to the line manager, whereas the corporate finance department has the expertise to handle the financial risks.

Business risks include competitor, technological and customer factors. Competitor risks are particularly important where a new product, sales outlet or pricing strategy is to be employed. If the project is going to have a significant impact on the market, it should be assumed that competitors will react if possible. How they react and how quickly may well be difficult to estimate and quantify. This factor must be considered and documented in the investment proposal, and if the possible reaction is going to be significant then contingency plans need to be built into the proposal. For example, if the new product is going to undercut competitors' prices by 20%, what will be done if the competitor responds with a corresponding 20% price reduction? How long can they afford to hold the lower price? Should we drop our price another 20%? What will this do to our cash flow?

For ventures into the unknown, the risk can be contained by the use of pilot projects that give a good indication of the likely success of the full project. The cost justification for a pilot project lies in its ability to minimize the risk of larger losses. It is worth spending $100,000 on a pilot for a $2 million project, but it is not worth spending it for a $200,000 project. Deciding what is, or is not, worthwhile is a subjective decision based on the extent of the possible risks and the ability properly to test the risks.

Complex Investment Proposals

Sometimes investment proposals are muddled and badly presented and I am tempted to throw them out without further consideration. This is dangerous as there may be a good idea hidden in the confusion.

Being a good businessman/woman or technician does not necessarily mean being good at coping with the forms and words needed to push an idea through the bureaucracy. Despite the intrinsic merit of the proposal, if it is poorly presented its chances of success will be unnecessarily diminished. Part of the role of the accountant is to assist in making sure the proposal is seen in the best light. Today there are numerous computer gadgets that facilitate high-class presentations. The quality of the presentation reflects directly on the presenter, and so it is worth the effort to produce a top-quality proposal.

Apart from the cosmetics of the proposal, there may be genuine inconsistencies that need to be ironed out before submission. For example, individual project proposals can often comprise two or more projects hidden under the one umbrella. Sometimes this is an intentional ploy to sneak in a pet project under the cover of some other activity, but more often it is a failure to observe that a proposal contains separable decisions. Disentangling complex proposals is necessary so as to clarify the real issues and to ensure that good ideas are not rejected because they are mingled with not-so-good ideas. The following investment proposal gives a simple example of the confusion of two separable decisions:

> We believe that a new branch in Main Street is very worthwhile, with strong growth potential and plenty of scope to obtain casual tourist customers. Buying the premises will cost $2.6 million and it will require $1.3 million to fit out, giving a payback of....

The decision to open the new branch is separable from the decision to buy the premises. Perhaps the new branch is worthwhile, but perhaps buying the premises is not the correct choice and it could be that the whole proposal is rejected solely because of the inappropriate suggestion to purchase the premises. The proposal and decision should be in two parts: namely, whether to open the branch, using market rental rates as the cost assumption; and what is the best way to accommodate the branch − whether to purchase, build or lease.

In contrast to the previous example, some proposals carry with them huge implications that are deliberately or erroneously omitted from the investment proposal. An example would be a proposal to change mainframe computers at a cost of $5 million. Omitted from the proposal is the implication that an additional $3 million will have to be spent to change the application systems software. Hopefully the senior executives would have sufficient experience to detect such a glaring anomaly. Having done so, future submissions from the same source are likely to be met with a fair degree of scepticism.

Financial Analysis

> We only get one chance to spend our money and we cannot afford to make a mess of that chance. If spending a few hours on a calculator is going to reduce the chance of wasting money, then it is time well spent.

Business investment decisions are seldom simple and usually require a mixture of quantitative and subjective evaluation. These quantitative measures are briefly explained subsequently. However, it must be recognized that such analyses are only as good as the raw data they use. Most astute managers recognize this and are fully capable of adjusting the assumptions to give the 'correct' answer. This does not invalidate the analysis totally, for it means that the project sponsor has had to think through the key assumptions and make an assessment of the business risks.

To evaluate a project financially, two types of analysis are relevant, namely *payback* and *discounted cash flow* (DCF). In a financial appraisal of a project, there may be cost–only analyses or there may be cost–benefit analyses. DCF copes with both categories, whereas payback is only relevant for projects that have quantifiable benefits or income that eventually exceeds costs.

Stay-in-business or strategic investments may defy quantification of their benefits. For investment in business expansion, productivity and new products, there are usually quantifiable benefits that allow a cost–benefit analysis using the payback or DCF techniques.

Unquantifiable Benefits

> It is easy to appraise a project that generates direct income. Many of our investments have no tangible income and I don't want the line managers wasting all our time by engaging in spurious cost–benefit studies.

Even in businesses where cost–benefit analyses are usually applicable, there will be numerous instances of projects with non-quantifiable benefits. For example, a supermarket chain may wish to invest in upgrading the shopping trolleys it provides for customer usage. The reason for the investment is a combination of corporate image, advertising potential and a reduction in repair costs, but it is not possible sensibly to quantify the benefits. The investment appraisal system must recognize that such projects will always occur and it has to be flexible enough to allow reasonable cost-only projects to have a fair chance of proceeding. Without this flexibility, sensible people make ridiculous estimates of benefits to substantiate an investment that they intuitively know is the right thing for the company to do.

Although a cost–benefit analysis for the shopping trolleys is not feasible, there may be different ways of providing the shoppers with the same service. These options should be translated into financial terms and compared to each other. If there is a significant difference in the timing of cash flow for the various options, then DCF can remove that factor and allow a fair comparison of the options.

Many of these cost–only projects are the result of corporate policy, an example being where the company specifies that all its customer reception areas must be decorated and furnished to exacting standards. In these cases, the costs are implied when the standards are set and the only question that remains is whether the additional customer reception space is really needed. This decision could be standardized as a formula based on customer traffic and waiting times. Once the decision has passed this test, there is no need for further financial analysis.

Payback Analysis

Discounted cash flow seems to be academically correct, but I feel that knowing the payback period is usually sufficient for making an informed decision.

Payback is a simple technique to understand, and it accords with the reality of many investment decisions in that it answers the question 'If I outlay some money, how long will it be before I get it back?' The longer it will take for the money to return, the more uncertainty exists because there is more chance of something going wrong. Uncertainty and risk are inherent in any business decision, and payback is a fair indicator of that uncertainty.

Figure 4.4 shows a simple payback calculation. In this example,

	Today	Year 1	Year 2	Year 3	Year 4	Year 5
Establishment costs	(100)					
Trading income		10	30	40	50	50
Annual cash flow	(100)	10	30	40	50	50
Cumulative cash flow	(100)	(90)	(60)	(20)	30	80
Payback Period	41 months			PAYBACK POINT		

Figure 4.4   Payback calculation example: establish new shop ($000)

sometime between the end of Year 3 and the end of Year 4 the cumulative cash position will turn from a deficit to a surplus. The proportion of the year can be estimated on a pro-rata basis, which in this case is 20/50 × 12 months, which is about 5 months. Thus the payback period is estimated to be 3 years + 5 months = 41 months.

The payback method does not worry about any income that occurs after the payback point, but this is a factor that may alter the overall decision to invest. The tax effect of the investment can affect the payback period if the project costs and income have different treatment for tax purposes. For example, the capital expenditure may only be claimable over a period of several years, if at all, whereas the income will be assessable in the year it is received. Therefore the tax effect of the cash flows should preferably be included in the cash flow statement. However, if both expenditure and income have an identical tax treatment, the tax effect can be ignored.

Discounted Cash Flow Analysis

I am sure that discounted cash flow is the correct way to go but I feel nervous when I have to explain an investment proposal to the board using mathematics that I don't really understand.

Discounted cash flow is an undeniably correct financial analysis technique that recognizes the timing effect of cash flows. It is suitable for evaluating projects where there is a long time lag between making the investment and receiving the benefits. A more detailed explanation of the DCF technique is given in the appendix to chapter 6. DCF analysis results in a figure called the *net present value* or the *internal rate of return*. The net present value (NPV) is the current worth of the project after adjusting for the fact that money payable or receivable in the future has a smaller value than money in the hand today – because of the alternative possibility of investing that money and earning interest.

While DCF is an elegant technique in concept, it has not received full acceptance. The main problem lies in traditional accounting concepts whereby business performance is expressed in terms of profit and historical asset values. These two concepts are at odds with NPV measurements. So long as profit continues as the primary measure of business performance, NPV will always have difficulty in gaining full acceptance. This is understandable in that businesses want to know how their investment is going to translate into profits and NPV cannot provide this information. The NPV figure is abstract and it will never appear in the financial accounts in any recognizable form.

Even though there is this obstacle, NPV is still a concept worth adopting as it provides an objective test. If the NPV is positive, the proposal can be said to have passed the test. The example in figure 4.5 shows an analysis of whether it is worthwhile to invest in a new truck. The project has an NPV of $9,155, which means that the investor is better off doing this project than leaving the money in total security in the bank and earning 12%. If the NPV were negative, the analysis would indicate that it was preferable to deposit the money in the bank at 12% interest.

The convention in this type of analysis is that initial cash outlays are considered to occur all on one day at the start of the project: this is presented as Y(0) or Year(0) in most analyses. Thereafter, all cash flows are considered to occur on the last day of subsequent years and this is presented as Y(1), Y(2), Y(3), etc. Obviously income and costs occur continuously throughout the year. However, some simplification is necessary and it will not usually distort the NPV result to any great extent to assume that all cash flows occur at a year end. The normal convention is that cash outlays are shown as negatives, ($10 million), and cash receipts are shown as positives, $10 million.

The DCF analysis does not include funding aspects such as borrowings for the project or loan repayments and interest. The

	Total	Today	Year 1	Year 2	Year 3	Year 4
Purchase new truck		(99,000)				
Income			68,500	68,500	68,500	68,500
Running costs			(38,000)	(39,000)	(40,000)	(35,000)
Sell truck						55,000
Taxation			(11,590)	(5,567)	(5,187)	(1,087)
Net cash flow		($99,000)	$18,910	$23,933	$23,313	$87,413
Discount factor @ 12%		1.000	0.893	0.797	0.712	0.636
Discounted cash flow	$9,155	($99,000)	$16,887	$19,075	$16,599	$55,595
Net Present Value	$9,155			Internal Rate of Return	15.33%	

Figure 4.5   Net present value example: purchase of new truck ($000)

interest element is reflected in the discount factor, and the inherent value of the project has to be divorced from how it is funded. Having decided that the project is worthwhile at a 12% discount rate, the next step is for the corporation's finance department to go and organize sufficient funds, preferably costing less than 12%.

The discount rate or hurdle rate will usually be expressed on an after-tax basis because of the differing tax treatments for equity and debt costs. Therefore the calculation of the cash flows should also be on an after-tax basis. This means doing a tax effect calculation for the project to identify the impact of tax and including the tax payments or benefits in the cash flow statement.

The discount rate partly reflects current interest rates, which in turn reflect inflation. To be consistent, the cash flow projections should also reflect inflation. Usually it is easier to use a discount rate that excludes the inflation factor in interest rates, so allowing use of cash flow projections that ignore inflation.

Since business executives find the NPV test too abstract, the alternative approach of internal rate of return (IRR) is used. IRR is another way of expressing the NPV test. The mathematics involve doing trial and error calculations to find the discount rate at which the project just passes the NPV test.

Referring again to the new truck example in figure 4.5, the IRR for the set of cost and income assumptions is 15.3%. This says that if the bank offered 14.9% interest on an investment, it would still be preferable to buy the truck. This is a much easier result for the layman to understand. By a quirk of mathematics, on rare occasions it is possible to have two IRRs that are equally true. One of the IRRs is likely to be an outlandish possibility and can be readily ignored.

The IRR is used in comparison to a hurdle rate that is set by the company to weed out unacceptable investment proposals. Thus, if the hurdle rate is 14% and the trucking project has an IRR of 15%, then it can be said that the proposal passes the company's hurdle rate. In both the NPV and the IRR methods there has to be a decision on the discount or hurdle rate that will be used. This is a major topic in itself and is briefly covered in the appendix to chapter 6.

Another indicator exists, known as the *financial rate of return*. It gives the investor an indication of the project's effect on the traditional accrual accounts. It is a waste of time and serves only to highlight the shortcomings of conventional ways of measuring a business. The example in figure 4.6 shows the calculations.

	Year 1	Year 2	Year 3	Year 4	Average
Historical asset cost	100	100	100	100	
Accumulated depreciation	(15)	(30)	(45)	(60)	
Net book value	85	70	55	40	63
Trading profit	10	25	26	28	
Less: Depreciation	(15)	(15)	(15)	(15)	
Profit before interest and tax	(5)	10	11	13	7
Financial rate of return	−5.9%	14.3%	20.0%	32.5%	11.1%

Figure 4.6   Financial rate of return example: establish new branch ($000)

Note: The rate of return is increasing each year partly because of a declining asset value.

However, it should be stressed that there are a number of variations on this method of calculation. In this example, the financial rate of return increases rapidly each year, which demonstrates the impossibility of making any sense of the analysis.

Application of Financial Analysis

I want to institute a standard investment test throughout the group so that we are all talking the same language. If the test is good enough for one business unit, then it's good enough for the rest of them.

Making investment choices is essentially management of business risks, which vary greatly from one type of business or industry to another. Three examples at different parts of the risk spectrum show the application of financial analysis to investment appraisal. The examples demonstrate how these three types of business would evaluate their investment options and, in particular, whether they would use DCF, payback or intuition.

Minerals Prospector

A minerals prospecting company looks for likely areas of mineral deposits and then invests millions of dollars in a drilling programme. The key to this business is the initial survey that gives an indication of the probability of mineral deposits. There may be failure, but if there is success then the financial results could be spectacular.

The minerals prospector has its own methodology for estimating the probability of finding the mineral reserves based on geological surveys. Using this probability it sets a limit on the project cost which may be amended according to subsequent drilling results. The company has to be brave enough to be able to admit defeat and walk away from the empty holes, and also brave enough to keep going in the face of repeated failure. DCF or payback techniques would not be of any help to the company in its investment decisions. The benefits are just too speculative to warrant the use of strict financial appraisal techniques.

Building Developer

A developer of suburban shopping centres looks for expanding suburbs and when the suburb matures is able to sell the shopping complex it has developed to institutional investors. If it picks a slow-moving suburb, the investment may yield only 8% per annum return over five years, whereas a dynamic suburb may yield 20% per annum over same period. There is a reasonable element of risk, which all depends on the initial siting.

The building developer lives by the effective rental yield on the shops it builds. It knows that the market capitalizes rents at, say, 10% and so if it can obtain rents of $500,000 per annum it can sell the shops for $5 million, compared with a cost of $3 million. It has to calculate the present value of $5 million and compare it with the initial outlay of $3 million plus the rents it receives, which is effectively a DCF calculation, as shown in figure 4.7.

Using this model, the building developer can trial the proposal various ways, looking at rental growth rate possibilities or the maximum site investment allowable to give a worthwhile return. Once the investment has been made, the model can still be used to decide on the timing of the sale, as the developer has to balance the cost of funding the investment against the prospective growth in value of the building that results from rental growth.

Supermarket Chain

A national chain of supermarket stores does meticulous market research to identify a new site. The supermarket chain has

	Total	Today	Year 1	Year 2	Year 3	Year 4	Year 5
Building cost		(3.00)					
Rental income			0.30	0.35	0.45	0.50	0.50
Sale proceeds							5.00
Net cash flow		(3.00)	0.30	0.35	0.45	0.50	5.50
Discount factor @ 12%		1.000	0.893	0.797	0.712	0.636	0.567
Discounted cash flow	1.31	(3.00)	0.27	0.28	0.32	0.32	3.12
Net Present Value $1.31				Internal Rate of Return		22%	

Figure 4.7 Building developer net present value: shopping complex development ($m)

numerous existing stores from which it can build up a profile of the factors that indicate whether a new store will be successful. Having narrowed the options down to a small number of potential sites, financial projections are made for each site showing the capital outlay and the annual contribution for the first three or four years. The risk of failure is relatively low, in view of the extensive experience that the company has in numerous other stores.

The evaluation of projected financial returns could be done by expressing contribution as a percentage of the investment. However, a timing element has to be introduced as some stores may take a while to build up a regular customer base. This could be expressed as 'The shop should be capable of making a 23% return on investment within two years', or better still it could be expressed as a maximum payback period: 'Investments that have a payback period of less than fifty-five months are acceptable.' This type of test ignores the income that will occur after the payback period. However, that is normally irrelevant to the decision as all possible sites for the supermarket would have similar lives and priority would be given to those sites with the quickest payback.

The use of NPV or IRR appraisal techniques could also be a help, but as the payback test has already done the job further analysis is not needed. The payback criterion effectively carries with it a required rate of return and in this example suits the investment decision that has to be made.

5

Business Valuation

It is tempting to buy an established business because there is more certainty about the investment. The chemistry of the assets and customers and staff have already been mixed together and, although some premium has to be paid for the work involved in assembling the pieces of the business, at least the success of that mixture is visible.

A business is a mix of assets that can generate cash for the owner. For purposes of business valuation, there are two ways of looking at the value of this bundle of assets and it is a matter of deciding on which method suits the circumstances. The two methods of valuing a business are:

- calculation of the liquidation value by reference to the cash that can be realized by selling off the assets;
- capitalization of future cash flows.

There is accounting jargon that refers to a valuation in terms of *net tangible assets* or multiples of current or historical profits. These are merely ways of expressing the value already calculated by one of the two methods listed above. There is absolutely no logic in buying a business in the expectation of future profits and basing that valuation on past experiences. The only thing that matters is the future.

Valuation Methods

We have expanded by buying several established businesses in recent years. We find that the published accounts for potential acquisitions are of very limited use when trying to establish a purchase price.

The cash-generating ability of the company could be viewed in terms of a liquidation of the existing assets or a continuation of normal trading. The liquidation view is normally inappropriate as the sum of the parts of a business should usually be worth much more than a quick sale of the individual parts: that is, the best option available to the investor is for the business to continue as a *going concern*.

In accounting, 'assets' is a narrow term that usually only describes items that have been purchased for cash. Accounting assets ignore many very valuable assets such as patents, trademarks, customer loyalty, corporate image, staff skills and product lines. When a business is purchased the whole bundle of assets is acquired, both the accounting assets and the unrecorded assets. It is not usually useful to think of the assets as separable items, although sometimes there are spare assets that could be sold off to realize cash while allowing the substance of the business to continue. A conventional balance sheet is in no way a representation of the value of a business, mainly because it ignores certain assets and the chemistry of their mixture, and also because the assets it does record are normally shown at their historical purchase price.

In rare cases a business has to be valued in terms of its liquidation value. Then the valuer has to consider how much each separable asset would yield on the open market. Total liquidation of a business is a last resort and is a good indicator that the chemistry of the assets has failed and has no value. To demonstrate the ways of valuing a business, consider the company whose financial results are shown in figure 5.1.

Valuation Based on Liquidation   Although the latest balance sheet shows net assets of $76 million, if the business were to be broken up and sold piece by piece, a vastly different result would occur. For example:

- The goodwill, book value $16 million, might be worth $5 million as the trademarks that it refers to have become unfashionable.
- The fixed assets, book value $110 million, would have minimal resale value as they represent highly specialized plant that would only suit a small number of buyers.
- The stock, book value $15 million, would probably have minimal resale value unless sold in the ordinary course of business. Once the liquidation of the company starts, many customers might abandon the company, making it difficult to move the stock.
- The $10 million owed by debtors would mostly be recovered, albeit slowly once they realized there would be no continuing

Balance Sheet

		Year 0
Goodwill	20	
Less: Amortization	(4)	16
Fixed assets	152	
Less: Depreciation	(42)	110
Stock		15
Debtors		10
Less: Trade creditors		(25)
Less: Debt		(50)
Net Assets		76

Profit History

	Year −2	Year −1	Year 0
Sales	155	176	200
Expenses	(134)	(155)	(172)
Depreciation and amortization	(9)	(10)	(10)
Interest	(4)	(5)	(6)
Tax	(3)	(3)	(5)
Profit after tax	5	3	7

Figure 5.1   Rising Star Opticals: financial results ($m)

business relationship. The $25 million owing to trade creditors would have to be repaid in full, as would the $50 million owing to lenders.

- Many liquidation expenses would occur, such as redundancy payments to long-serving staff.

In this example the liquidation of the company might realize only $10 million instead of the $76 million shown as the net assets in the balance sheet.

Going Concern Valuation   If the business is to be kept going, then the net assets valuation of $76 million shown in the balance sheet is a totally arbitrary basis for setting the purchase price. As a going concern, the valuation has to reflect future profits or cash flow. Profit is a hybrid concept that most people deem to be synonymous with cash flow. In some cases this can be so, but often there is a marked divergence between profits and cash flow and it is future cash flow that is important. It would be an unwelcome surprise to buy a profitable business and then find that it needed huge quantities of cash to sustain its growth or just to replace outdated equipment.

Usually the purchase price of a business exceeds the balance sheet value of its assets. In accounting jargon, the difference between the actual price paid for a business and its net assets is termed *goodwill*. For some inexplicable reason, the accounting standards require the purchaser to write off goodwill over ten years or less. Sometimes net assets can be a reasonable basis for negotiation, but only where the company holds monetary assets, such as bonds, which have been recorded at their market values. Inevitably the market value reflects the future income attached to those monetary assets. It is entirely fallacious to think that valuing a business concerns acceptance of the balance sheet values and then bargaining around the valuation of goodwill as some sort of premium that has to be paid over and above the 'true' value of the business.

There is an active market for the purchase and sale of complete businesses. In the market, the practice is to express the purchase price as a multiple of current profits. The size of this multiple reflects the market's optimism about the future. For example, a business with prospects of 20% annual growth in earnings might sell for twenty times its current earnings, and a business with a 15% annual growth in earnings might sell for twelve times its current earnings. These are just broad indicators of what is happening in a competitive market, and they define an approximate price range in which a deal might be struck in a competitive bidding situation.

This does not mean that the purchaser merely has to forecast profit growths and multiply current profits by a multiple obtained from the local stockbroker. Purchasers have to make their own decision about what the business is worth to them. Whether they then bother to make a bid will depend on whether they think that, given the current market for buying and selling businesses, they can make the purchase for less than or equal to their own valuation of the business. This is the difference between speculation and the making of an informed decision.

When valuing a business, it is worth stressing the difference between its potential value and its current value. A simple example of a city car park will suffice. At present, the operator of a car park in the middle of the city charges $1 per day for parking and the present value of this stream of income is only $100,000. However, if the car park operator were a bit more astute, he could put up a multi-storey car park and charge $20 per day for ten times as many car spaces. The present value of this option is $5 million.

There is a large discrepancy between the potential value of the business ($5 million) and its value under existing management practices ($100,000). The purchaser of this business is interested in the existing cash flow from the business, as it sets the base purchase price. The purchaser is also vitally interested in the potential cash flow and there will have to be estimates of the probability of gaining planning permission to build the new multi-storey car park. This probability will radically affect the purchase price, which may be anywhere between $100,000 and $5 million.

Even if planning permission is assured, the purchaser would be silly to pay the full $5 million to the previous owner. That price would mean that all the value added in the car park development had passed to the previous owner and not to the investor who stood by the risk during the construction phase.

Valuing Growth

> The accountant says we should bid $2 per share based on historical earnings trends. The sales manager says we should bid $4 per share as the business has tremendous sales opportunities. The engineering manager says we shouldn't touch it, as all their equipment is out of date. Somewhere, there has to be a rational price?

To value a business the business activities have to be looked at in detail and the sustainable cash flow has to be estimated. Having done this, the next step is to translate that future cash flow into a spot value that can be used for negotiating. This is similar in concept to the DCF technique popularly used for investment appraisals. The mathematics are not hard, but the valuer needs sound experience in that type of industry to make a reasonable prediction of future cash flow.

Since the published statutory accounts are of very limited use in valuing a business, access to more detailed information can radically affect the offer price as it gives more certainty about future cash flows. No doubt the vendor will try to impress on the purchaser the latent potential in the business, and the valuer has to assess the probability of the business plans and strategies actually occurring. For instance, if one of the major valuation assumptions concerns the introduction of a new product next year, then the valuer must find out whether the product development is on schedule and whether the schedule will actually allow delivery of a new product next year. The valuer also has to look at the industry to see if there are any major trends that need to be reflected in the cash flow forecast. For example, if the industry is under threat from cheap imports, then there would have to be an assessment of how this will affect trading margins. The valuer must have a high degree of relevant industry experience in order to understand the strategies and business practices of the company being valued. Industry and government statistics can be used to determine expected overall economic growth, sectorial growth, labour availability and inflation.

Continuing with the example that was shown in figure 5.1, a cash flow forecast is shown in figure 5.2. Only the first four years are shown, although in theory the purchaser expects the cash to keep flowing in perpetuity, a mathematical difficulty that will be covered later.

To prepare this cash flow forecast, various assumptions were needed, such as sales growth, profit margins and the capital expenditure needed to sustain that growth. It could be that, for a cheap acquisition, a payback indicator might give the purchaser sufficient comfort to make a bid. He might be able to say to himself, 'It is highly likely that I can buy this company for $85 million and I estimate that this would be paid back out of net cash flow within five years. That sounds reasonable and I will negotiate around the $85 million price range.' But a business with good growth potential is likely to sell for a longer payback period than five years and a DCF analysis is more appropriate. This brings back the problem of having to assume that cash flows continue into the indefinite future.

Even in a high-growth business there has to be the assumption that the growth inherent in the business when it was purchased will eventually stop. There may be growth *ad infinitum*, but this will occur as a result of the skill of the new management and is not

Cash Flow Forecast

	Next year	Next year +1	Next year +2	Next year +3	Every year thereafter
Sales	224	258	296	326	326
Expenses	(189)	(218)	(250)	(275)	(275)
Capital expenditure	(16)	(18)	(15)	(10)	(10)
Tax payments	(8)	(10)	(13)	(20)	(20)
Net cash flow	11	12	18	21	21

Valuation Based on Future Cash Flow

	Future value	12% Discount factor	Present value
Next year cash flow	11	0.893	10
Next year +1 cash flow	12	0.797	10
Next year +2 cash flow	18	0.712	13
Next year +3 cash flow	21	0.636	13
Constant cash flows received forever	21	5.300	111
			156
Plus: Proceeds from sale of spare assets			2
Less: Assumed repayment of existing debt			(50)
Present Value of the Business			108

Figure 5.2   Rising Star Opticals: cash flow forecast and valuation ($m)

Note: The above forecast ignores interest costs. The perpetual cash flows are capitalized at 12% ($21 m/0.12 = $175m), which is then discounted to present values by a factor of 0.636 ($175m × 0.636 = $111m). The $108m valuation is approximately 15 times current earnings.

something that has to be paid for in the purchase price. It could well be that any purchased growth has only three or four years to run. Such an assumption is not only logical and realistic, but it also greatly simplifies the rationale for the purchase price.

Therefore, when preparing the cash flow forecast, it is only necessary to forecast for the number of years where profits are deemed to be increasing because of the intrinsic value of the business when it was acquired. In practical terms, this limit would not exceed four years and could be less. So there is only the need to forecast the cash flow over the next four years, and thereafter the assumption is that the cash flows that exist in the fourth year will continue for ever. In DCF mathematical terms, it means that the fourth year's cash flow is treated as a perpetual stream of income (a perpetuity) and the programmable calculator can handle this quite easily.

As a result of the DCF calculation in the previous example, it is estimated that the business has an NPV of $156 million. Furthermore, it has surplus assets that could be sold for $2 million without any damage to future cash flows. The cost of repaying existing debt is deducted, since the cash flow forecast assumed that no interest costs would be incurred. This gives a maximum value to the purchaser of $108 million, which is fifteen times current earnings levels. Similar businesses have sold for only ten to twelve times current earnings and so there definitely seems to be scope for putting in a competitive bid that will allow a long-term gain. The purchaser starts the bargaining at $84 million (twelve times earnings) and sets his top price at $100 million, which would be fourteen times current earnings.

From this point onwards the bargaining gets involved in financial engineering with schemes to swap debt for equity or to make deferred payments. These are merely ways of trying to extract concessions on the purchase price or to spread the risk. They do not alter the fundamental assessment of the worth of the acquisition.

Application of Valuation Techniques

It is no good just buying a business and sitting on it – you might as well put the money in the stock market, at least then you can get hold of the money again quickly. If you are going to buy a business, you have to be able to see an opportunity to add to the value of the business.

The following three examples demonstrate variations on the theme of purchasing an existing business. For each of these examples, the decision required is 'What is the top price I would be willing to pay?' Once this has been decided, the wheeling and dealing starts in an attempt to secure the purchase for less than the top price.

Even if not actively seeking to purchase an existing business, it is worth understanding the thought processes in case someone offers to buy your business. Then it may be possible to work out what is the purchaser's top price and so ensure you extract that price as part of the negotiations. Or it may be possible to seek out another purchaser who has different opportunities for enhancing the acquired business and thus may have a higher top price.

Small Fry–Quick Fry Merger

In this example, there is the intention to merge two businesses and so there has to be a consideration of the merger costs and the result of the combined operation. This example uses the concept of capitalizing earnings to give a present value: by knowing the earnings and the required rate of return, it is simple mathematics to calculate the value. Thus if a 10% return is needed and profits are $10, then the investment is worth $100 ($10/10%). The example also tries to demonstrate some strategic angles of buying a business.

Quick Fry has 20% of the cooking oil market. Its main competitor, Deep Fry, has 30% of the market. Another minor competitor, Small Fry, has 15% of the market and is finding it hard to compete. As a result it is suffering low profitability and its owners are willing to sell the business at a reasonable price. Deep Fry has just invested heavily in new equipment with the intention of cutting costs and improving its grip on the market. It does not want to buy Small Fry as it has limited access to additional funds because of its recent expenditure, but it is willing to put in a bid just to make sure Small Fry is not sold too cheaply. Deep Fry must be careful that its bid is not successful, as it does not want to be saddled with any more management problems, more debt or irate stockholders.

Quick Fry sees the acquisition of Small Fry as the only way to stop Deep Fry from dominating the market. The bid price will have to be sensible but low enough to make the whole exercise worthwhile. It sends in a team to look at the books of Small Fry. They produce the cash flow projection shown in figure 5.3, which assumes that the merged market share stays at 35%, that per unit costs decrease by 12% because of economies of scale in marketing

	Year −2	Year −1	Year 0	Year 1	Year 2	Year 3
Small Fry	2.0	2.2	2.3			
Quick Fry	5.5	6.0	6.5			
Merger costs				−2.5	−2.0	
Combined operation				9.3	10.8	12.5
Cash Flow	7.5	8.2	8.8	6.8	8.8	12.5

Figure 5.3   Small Fry–Quick Fry merger: cash flow projection ($m)

Note: Assumes (1) no market share will be lost during the merger, (2) production economies will reduce operating costs by 12%.

and purchasing, and that successful implementation of the merger will cost $4.5 million over two years.

Therefore its cash flow will increase from $6.5 million per annum to $12.5 million per annum, an increase of $6 million per annum. Its cost of capital is 15%, and so the maximum potential price is $35.5 million, calculated as follows:

($6 million/15%) = $40 million minus $4.5 million in merger costs
= $35.5 million

The first test is to see whether Small Fry is likely to accept this price. $35 million values Small Fry at about fifteen times its current earnings ($35 million/$2.3 million), which is quite generous considering Small Fry's earnings are likely to decline if Deep Fry starts its price war. This price also leaves no value for Quick Fry investors to reward them for the downside risks, in particular that market share is lost during the merger. It is decided to put in an opening bid of $25 million with an upper limit of $30 million should the bidding go that far.

Meanwhile, Deep Fry has its sums all wrong and puts in an opening spoiling bid of $40 million. Quick Fry cannot match this bid and so the Deep Fry bid is accepted. Deep Fry then has to borrow heavily to pay for the acquisition and for the costs of implementing the merger. Within a year, interest rates have risen by 5% and Deep Fry has severe cash flow problems. Quick Fry came out of the exercise unscathed because it had decided on its top price and then had the courage to stick to it, even though it was very keen to make the purchase. When Quick Fry was doing its calculations of the financial benefits of the merger, the estimate was that the full benefits would take two years to flow into improved profits. It could have adjusted for this timing effect by discounting future benefits, but the change in values would have been relatively small and the increased sophistication was not warranted.

Bargain Basements

This example looks at the break-up value of business. The time spans are short and so discounting future cash flows does not add to the decision process.

A far-sighted shopkeeper built up an empire of small shops in the Depression years that is now owned by his grandson. The business, known as Bargain Basements, has evolved into two segments, low-priced clothes and health foods, mostly housed in premises that have been owned for sixty years. The grandson has joined a religious cult and wishes to make a large donation. He has instructed his lawyers to sell the business by tender within the next three months.

The Opportunity Corporation is interested in the possibilities of separating the real estate from the trading operations and thereby making a quick return. They summarize the statutory accounts of Bargain Basements for the past three years as shown in figure 5.4. Clearly the business is worth more than the net assets of $15.4 million as it is making profits of $10 million per annum. Valued on a rate of return of 15%, these profits would be worth a purchase price of about $65 million ($10 million/15%). It may yet be worth more.

A valuation of the properties indicates that they have a market worth of approximately $185 million at current prices. If they had charged rent to the business units at commercial rates, the operating statement would be as shown in the segmented profit report in figure 5.4.

This indicates that the retailing segments of the business could not survive if they were charged with a commercial rate of rent. In terms of a prospective purchaser, they have little value unless their performance can be turned around by a specialist in the retailing industry. Opportunity Corporation decides to involve a joint venture partner to see what can be done with the retailing segments. It is thought that the clothing business has no hope and would have to be closed. The food business could be improved to generate $2 million per annum in pre-tax profits, making it worth about $15 million, but only after $10 million has had to be invested by the new owner. Therefore its maximum present value is about $5 million.

The estimated liquidated value of the company is shown in figure 5.4. This estimates that a purchase price of $135 million would give a profit of $24 million and this would represent a 17% return for the risk of making a $135 million investment.

Opportunity Corporation's strategy is to sell off the properties

Figure 5.4   Bargain Basements: financial results ($m)

Balance Sheet

	Year −2	Year −1	Year 0
Buildings at cost	5.0	4.9	4.8
Stock at cost	11.0	11.1	11.2
Debtors and cash	0.5	0.6	0.7
Assets	16.5	16.6	16.7
Less: Debt and creditors	(1.1)	(1.2)	(1.3)
Net Assets	15.4	15.4	15.4

Income Statement

	Year −2	Year −1	Year 0
Operating Income	15.0	19.0	20.0
Tax	(5.0)	(6.0)	(10.0)
Net Profit After Tax	10.0	13.0	10.0

Segmented Profit Report for the Latest Year

	Food	Clothes	Property	Total
Operating income	15.0	5.0		20.0
Internal rents	(15.0)	(9.0)	24.0	0.0
Segment Income	0.0	(4.0)	24.0	20.0

Figure 5.4 cont.

Profitability Estimates and Actual Results

	Original estimate	Actually realized
Sale of buildings	186	168
Sale of food business	15	12
Less: Enhancement costs	(10)	(11)
Sale of clothing business	0	5
Less: Enhancement costs		(2)
Less: Closing-down costs	(5)	
Acquisition expenses	(7)	(10)
Interest costs (assumed 100% funded by debt)	(20)	(15)
Net proceeds	159	147
Less: Purchase price	(135)	(140)
Profit	24	7
Profit as % of Outlay	17%	5%

over the next year to property investors once long-term tenants have been found for the clothing shops. This has a degree of risk in that the property market may fall in that time. Opportunity Corporation assesses that it needs a pre-tax return of 15% on its investment to make the risk worthwhile.

The 15% is a broad estimate that takes into account the risk of the property market moving in the wrong direction or of having to hold the properties for a long time, so incurring high interest costs. Since there are so many permutations, it is unlikely that fine-tuning the calculation is going to give a better insight into what is a reasonable price to pay.

As it turns out, Opportunity Corporation pays $140 million for the business, and after it has effected its liquidation strategy the profit on the deal is $7 million: the details are also shown in figure 5.4.

The profit that the purchaser made from the deal could well have been made by the original owner if he had perceived that he had three separable businesses instead of just two. Instead, it was not until an outsider came into the business that the full value was released, partly to the original owner and partly to the purchaser. Because the time spans for the business strategy were short (one year), there was no need to consider DCF. However, once time spans lengthen, the need for the discounting of future cash flows becomes more relevant.

Luxury Lagoon

This example considers the acquisition of a half-finished project where a new investor has to look at the costs required to take the project through to completion. The sunk costs are irrelevant to the purchase price. The new investor has to ensure that the new scheme for profit sharing provides a reward for the risks involved and motivation for a passive shareholder whose participation is vital to future success.

Luxury Lagoon is a half-finished hotel on a remote Pacific island, being built to coincide with completion of an international airport which will bring in many tourists. The hotel is owned by a consortium of private investors and the island government. Delays, cost escalation and political turmoil have stalled the proj-

---

Current Balance Sheet

Assets
Land sold by government	2
Development costs to date	7
	9

Financed by
External investors' equity	7
Government loan (interest free)	2
	9

Figure 5.5a Luxury Lagoon: balance sheet ($m)

Investment Calculation

	NPV @13%	Y1	Y2	Y3	Y4	Y5	Y6	Y7	Y(8)
Stage One									
Costs to complete		(5.0)	(3.0)	(1.0)					
Operating income				1.0	2.0	3.0	3.0	3.0	
Tax							(1.5)	(1.5)	
		(5.0)	(3.0)	0.0	2.0	3.0	1.5	1.5	→
	2.3								
Stage Two									
Development costs				(2.0)	(1.0)				
Operating income						1.0	2.0	2.5	
Tax							(1.0)	(1.3)	
				(2.0)	(1.0)	1.0	1.0	1.3	→
	3.8								
Total	6.1								

Figure 5.5b Luxury Lagoon: investment calculation ($m)

Note: Cash flows after year 7 have been assumed to occur for ever. If the tax holiday were extended to seven years, the NPV would increase to $8.5 million.

ect and none of the participants can afford any more capital. They have approached Oceanic Operators to buy them out and complete the hotel. So Oceanic has to assess what price would make the deal worthwhile. The balance sheet for the hotel venture is shown in figure 5.5.

The government loan is interest free for the next five years and then convertible into equity. The profits from the hotel will be free of tax for the first five years. The hotel is to be built in two stages so that it can be enlarged as the tourist trade increases. The cash flow forecast for the project over the next seven years is shown in figure 5.5.

The historical sunk costs on the hotel are irrelevant to the prospective purchaser. Although $7 million has already been spent on building work, another $9 million is required to complete stage one and a further $3 million for the later stage. The main criteria are the future costs and future income and, because these stretch a long way into the future, discounting is required to eliminate the timing effect of the cash flows. The net present value of the investment for both stages is $6 million, based on a cost of capital of 13%, which is the after-tax rate relevant to this international hotel operator. The $6 million represents the top price that an informed new investor would pay.

The project has been plagued by problems so far but Oceanic Operators are skilled in this type of business and think they can successfully complete the hotel. They negotiate with the investors to buy them out for $4 million in cash: if Oceanic are going to put in all the cash needed to finish the project, they do not want to have to share any of the future profits. The original investors have lost money, receiving only $4 million after investing $7 million, but it could have been worse – they might not have found any buyer.

Having removed the external investors, the next step is to arrange suitable terms with the island government as it is essential to give the government a strong vested interest and to insulate it from political embarrassment. One bargaining position is to try and extend the tax-free holiday on the project. The DCF analysis is run again assuming a seven-year tax holiday and this increases the present value by $2.4 million, all of which is attributable to the island government. After some bargaining, the government accepts $3 million in cash, extends the tax-free period to seven years and receives an option to purchase 10% of the equity in the company at any time, using a valuation from an independent arbitrator. Without quantifying the financial potential of the project, it would not be possible to strike a rational price and to negotiate around that price.

6

Project Control

Having decided to proceed with a project, the next step is to control the work and costs such that the project is successful and completed within financial constraints. Therefore a system is required to monitor physical progress and expenditure. Monitoring of historical costs is useful in imposing managerial accountability but, more importantly, knowledge of the costs-to-complete is essential to ensure that the project remains viable.

A project is a piece of work with a start date and an end date. It is separable from normal routine operations and is usually instigated to impose some change on the existing business. Each project must have an 'owner' or sponsor who has responsibility for ensuring the success of the project. The owner of the project

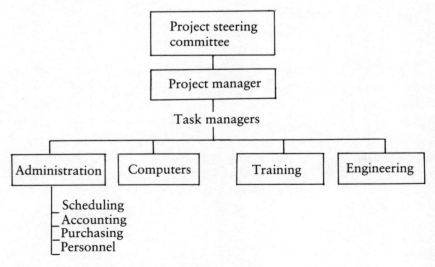

Figure 6.1   Large project organization chart

may delegate certain aspects to a project manager to supervise the technical work, sometimes using external consultants or technical contractors.

Large projects may have an organization structure of their own, and figure 6.1 shows the structure for a sample project. In this structure, a steering committee has been established to ensure co-ordination of the project across inter-divisional organization boundaries. In this type of structure, the project manager should prepare monthly or quarterly progress reports for the steering committee which communicate the status of the project and, in particular, whether it will be completed on schedule and within the financial budget.

The project manager in turn needs information from the task managers on how their part of the project is progressing. The administration function has to support the smooth running of the project as well as the reporting to the project manager and from the project manager to the steering committee. In a project large enough to warrant its own dedicated organization structure, dedicated accounting and scheduling systems would be needed.

Reporting Project Progress

Parts of our business are experts at managing projects while others, such as marketing and data processing, often don't even know they are running a project, let alone do it properly. If it's a good enough discipline for the engineers, then it is good enough for the administrators and support staff.

Some industries are project based and have extensive expertise in the planning and control of projects, the civil engineering industry being a prime example. Other industries undertake projects less frequently and, as a result, have little project management experience. They may not even realize they are conducting a separable project and the work may be totally immersed into routine operations with adverse consequences for both the project and normal day-to-day business.

Project control is the discipline of setting physical plans, and concomitant financial plans, and managing to those plans. The first step in setting a plan is progressively to break down the project into discrete tasks and to work out the dependencies of one task on another. Using the example of the implementation of a new computer system, the dependencies of one task to another are as shown in table 6.1.

Table 6.1

Task	Dependency
Software choice	Depends on technical needs
Hardware choice	Depends on software choice
Software ordering	Depends on software choice
Hardware ordering	Depends on hardware choice
Computer room refitting	Depends on hardware choice
Operator training	Depends on hardware testing
Hardware testing	Depends on computer room refitting
Software testing	Depends on hardware testing
Staff user training	Depends on software testing

As can be seen, each task depends on one or more proceeding tasks, and a delay in one task can flow through to others. In a large project there may be hundreds of tasks and sub-tasks with complex relationships. Analytical techniques have been developed for estimating the elapsed time required for a project. These techniques, *critical path analysis* and *PERT*, require logical analysis and calculation which is ideally suited to computer processing, and there are many pieces of computer software for such purposes. Of course, the scheduling system is only as good as the source data it receives, and so the project manager has to invest considerable time in analysing the project into logical tasks.

Apart from scheduling the tasks in the project, it is essential to monitor and control the risks of a project. The major risks should have been identified as part of the project approval process.

Financial control of the project has two main aspects: imposing accountability for expenditure and, most importantly, forecasting the future costs needed to complete the project.

Having broken up the project into individual tasks for scheduling purposes, it would be feasible to ascribe budgeted costs to each task. Before doing so, however, it is worth considering at what level cost control should be exercised. Historical costs are of relevance only for purposes of managerial accountability: that is, to require managers to explain why they spent the money. This can be achieved by looking at costs at a fairly high level of detail, not task by task, so saving the unnecessary effort of analysing project costs (employee time sheets, contractors' invoices, etc.) into minute detail. However, to prepare a reasonable forecast it is necessary to look at each task in detail and to estimate its future costs.

The popular computer software packages used for project management have the capacity to record the budgets and the actual costs of each task. While this seems like the best way to integrate project scheduling and cost reporting, the problem lies in trying to keep the actual cost data accurate. In practice, it may be more efficient to separate totally the project scheduling from the bookkeeping system. For example, in the project scheduling system there will be numerous operational tasks, such as 'sign contract', that have great significance in terms of the critical path for the project but no significance when recording actual costs. It is therefore impossible to have a one-for-one match between the tasks and the items of cost. The prime focus in a complex project has to be control over the operational tasks and their scheduling. If there is any chance of the bookkeeping process hindering the scheduling system, the bookkeeping has to be isolated from the scheduling system.

The reporting cycle for projects should follow the pattern shown in figure 6.2. Operational milestones are a set of key points in the project that are used to track actual progress. They should

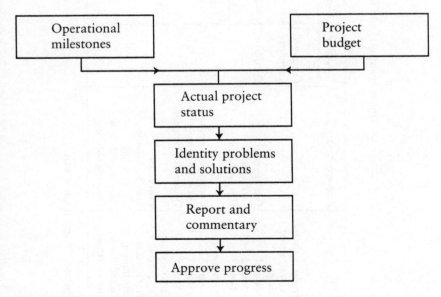

Figure 6.2   Project control process

Project: Spareparts Order Entry System   Status as at:.................

Task	Success criteria	October	November	December	January	February	March	April	May	June
Tender evaluated		Completed 15/6/-2								
Contract signed		Completed 18/7/-2								
Design:										
Stage 1	User approval	Completed 15/9/-2	X							
Stage 2	User approval			X						
Stage 3	User approval				X					
Programming:										
Stage 1	Documented programs			X						
Stage 2	Documented programs						X			
Stage 3	Documented programs			X						
Create test data	Passes tests				X					
Test programs	Transfer reconciled					X				
Transfer data	2% error rate						X			
User training	2 sec. response time							X		
Parallel running	2 sec. response time								X	
Live operation	1 sec. response time									X XXXXX

Figure 6.3   Project progress chart

be set in terms of time and performance standards, and the project progress chart in figure 6.3 demonstrates the concept. This type of report needs to be supported by technical status reports, as shown in figure 6.4, which advise interested parties of what is happening in detail. There also needs to be a financial report, such as the project cost summary shown in figure 6.5.

Task: Systems design – Stage 2 (backorder system)

Due date: 18/11/–2
Estimated completion date: 24/12/–2

At the August steering committee meeting it was decided to accept the revised user specification for backorders. This is radically different to their initial specification and will require 24 weeks of work to prepare a totally revised system design. Two contractors have been brought in to assist at an extra cost of $50,000. The milestone for the task will be delayed by 5 weeks. This will delay the whole project by 3 weeks. All project team leaders have been notified.

Signed _ _ _ _ _ _ _ _ _ _ _ _ _

Figure 6.4   Technical status report

These three types of report can be summarized and consolidated for high-level reporting according to the level of detail that the project owner or steering committee deems appropriate. The minimum they need to receive is:

- the actual costs incurred;
- the latest estimate of the total project cost;
- the project completion date;
- details of the technical success of the project.

Task	Costs already incurred	Costs to complete	Total costs	Project budget
Tender evaluated	50,123	0	50,123	60,000
Design				
Stage 1	184,567	0	184,567	230,000
Stage 2	80,321	120,000	200,321	85,000
Stage 3		90,000	90,000	90,000
Programming	29,900	350,000	379,900	390,000
Create test data		10,000	10,000	10,000
Test programs		70,000	70,000	10,000
Transfer data		10,000	10,000	12,000
User training		75,000	75,000	50,000
Parallel running		90,000	90,000	90,000
Live operation		150,000	150,000	100,000
Hardware	651,069	380,000	1,031,069	1,200,000
Total	995,980	1,345,000	2,340,980	2,327,000
	Expected Cost Variance			(13,980)

Figure 6.5   Project cost summary as at 31/10/X2

Sunk Costs

They are half way through the project and have spent 80% of the budget. I am tempted to disband the whole project as I am doubtful of their ability ever to achieve proper success. But $850,000 is an awful lot of money to have to write off to experience.

The cost component may appear to be of only minor interest once the project is in progress, as projects are not usually stopped part of the way through solely on financial grounds. However, financial accountability is a major consideration not only in the current project, but also as a message to all future project managers. Once it becomes common knowledge that the firm is not too worried about cost control, it will foster a culture of deliberately underestimating project costs (to assist in gaining approval for a project) in the comfort that actual costs are unimportant. An accurate historical record of project costs can also be a valuable benchmark when it comes to planning a similar type of project at some later date.

In projects that are experimental or unusual for that business, there is the possibility of massive cost overruns. Naturally, such projects have to be controlled by constantly looking at the future costs against the future benefits. When evaluating the future viability of a project, the business can become the captive of 'sunk costs' when the real decision centres on future costs. Sunk costs are those incurred from past actions and they may have resulted in little or no lasting value, particularly if the project has to be abandoned before completion. However, on some projects the business may say to itself, 'We've already spent $2 million. Let's keep going.' For this reason, in project reporting, sunk costs should keep a low profile with the emphasis being on future costs.

Part of the risk evaluation or the key assumptions used for justifying the project may contain factors that, if they radically change, alter the course of the project. For example, if the project is predicated on an oil price of $20 per barrel and it falls to $10 per barrel, then the whole project may have to be halted or scaled down. These key indicators have to be given a prominent role in the routine reporting for the project.

Project Control Guidelines

We have too many failures of projects to be delivered on schedule and within budget. We need some tight procedures for project control, and if the project fails the project manager cannot say he was not told how to do the job.

The general principles that apply to project control can be set in a series of guidelines which form part of the company's procedures. While this can be considered too bureaucratic, there is no point in waiting until the project has fallen into a hole before offering good advice on how it should have been managed. The guidelines can take the form of a manual which spells out every procedure, or merely a two-page statement of principles. The approach really depends on whether the projects are repetitive and the procedures can be accurately defined, in which case the large manual is appropriate, or whether the projects are irregular and general principles will need to be adapted to suit the circumstances.

The general principles that should be applied to project control are:

- there must be a clear specification of what the project is supposed to achieve, by when and at what cost;
- the eventual user of the results of the project must signify agreement to the project outputs specification;
- responsibility for ownership of the project and for project management must be clearly assigned;
- the business relationship with subcontractors (from both inside and outside the firm) should be properly documented and controlled;
- a formal project control and reporting system should be used;
- the user should formally accept delivery of the project at its completion;
- the project should be subject to a post-implementation review, say six months after completion.

By leaving the guidelines as a statement of general principles, the firm can be strict in ensuring widespread agreement. Defining all the steps in small detail will mean that the specifications will be lengthy and probably inappropriate to any one project in particular. Making detailed definitions of all procedures for a management role is a dangerous precedent as it gives the impression to the novice manager that the book contains all the answers, when the answers are really contained in a commonsense and businesslike approach to the task.

Defining Project Costs

This accounting system is ridiculous. It says we have only spent $30,000 on the project when I know I signed a $2.5 million supply contract only two weeks ago.

When the project manager asks 'How much have we spent?' there are a variety of possible answers, depending on what definitions apply to expenditure. The difficulty lies in deciding at what point a cost is recognized. Cost may be recognized on:

- authorization of the project: the money is effectively committed as it will not be used elsewhere;
- verbal agreement of terms with a supplier: there is a strong intention to pay and probably a legal liability as well;
- signing the supply contract or purchase order: there is a definite legal liability to pay;
- receipt of the goods or service: this is the normal accrual accounting definition of expenditure;

• payment of the money owing to the supplier: this is the cash accounting definition of expenditure.

Routine accounting systems attempt to recognize expenditure once the goods have been received, although in practice the processing of the supplier's invoice is the usual medium for recording expenditure. In a project, the preference is to consider expenditure to have occurred when the purchase order is raised. This is termed *commitment accounting*. While commitment accounting is helpful for project management, it is not an easy bookkeeping exercise.

The practical problems with commitment accounting are that:

• some purchase orders may not include any prices, requiring estimates that have to be amended once the real price is known: even for purchase orders with firm prices, the eventual cost may vary from that quoted;
• undocumented purchases are sure to occur which confuse the normal routine;
• the project costs are then measured on a basis different to the business's normal statutory accounts.

A commitment accounting system requires a very tight clerical control process in order to avoid turning into a bookkeeping mess. If there are any doubts about the ability to maintain that tight control, the project should use the traditional accrual accounting method.

When there needs to be a tight control of commitments, and there are doubts about whether a fully integrated commitments bookkeeping system can be maintained, it is better to keep a stand alone commitments register. The project manager can be told two figures: the accrual accounting expenditure and the committed expenditure. Whichever reporting method is being adopted, it has to be notified to all the users of the financial reports so that they are aware of what constitutes 'actual costs'.

Profit Recognition

The board keeps pestering me about the lack of profits from the big land drainage job we are doing. I keep telling them we only recognize profits once we have finished the job, but they still keep asking me the same question.

Firms that engage in projects for resale, such as civil engineering contractors, have to decide how and when they recognize profits and losses on the project. No doubt this is clearly spelled out in the firm's accounting standards, but it is worth looking at the various options. One approach, which is often used for small contracts, is to wait until the end of the contract before reporting any profit but to report potential total losses as soon as they are perceived to be likely to occur. This method is all right for small contracts, but for

---

Contract Cost Estimate

	Expected cost ($m)
Hydraulic surveys	2.6
Earthworks – Stage 1	4.7
Earthworks – Stage 2	3.2
Earthworks – Stage 3	8.6
Pipelaying	4.3
Pumping stations	2.8
Commissioning	3.9
Estimated costs	30.1
Profit	8.9
Total contract price	39.0

Contract Profit Recognition

	Expected total profit ($m)	Cumulative % of engineers' time	Reported cumulative profit ($m)
Hydraulic surveys	8.9	4	0.36
Earthworks – Stage 1	8.6	9	0.77
Earthworks – Stage 2	9.0	23	2.07
Earthworks – Stage 3	7.5	53	3.98
Pipelaying		63	
Pumping stations		81	
Commissioning		100	

Figure 6.6   Contract costs and estimated profits

Note: Periodically the total contract profit is re-forecast. Initially it was expected to be $8.9 million but the latest forecast is $7.5 million. Therefore $3.98 million is the profit earned so far ($7.5 million × 0.53).

long-term contracts the company will want to report some progressive profits to reassure its investors that no calamity has happened.

Consider an engineering contract, with its costs and estimated profits set out in figure 6.6. At the outset it expects to make a profit of $8.9 million on the whole contract. Since the project was priced according to overhead and profit recovery on a limiting factor, such as engineering manhours, it is logical to report profits according to the same formula. In figure 6.6 there is a second table that explains how profits are recognized during the contract. After the first task had been completed, it was thought that the total profits would still be $8.9 million. Since 4% of the expected limiting factor had been used, 4% of the expected profit should be reported.

After the fourth task had been completed, the total profit estimate had been revised downwards to $7.5 million. Since 53% of the limiting factor had been used, 53% of $7.5 million is reported as the cumulative profit. The profit for any one accounting period is the difference between the latest version of the cumulative profit and the profits already reported. In some cases this may be a loss if expected profits are revised sharply downwards.

A less scientific approach is progressively to report expected profits in proportion to the project costs. While this is simple, it does not necessarily reflect the stages in the project where the contractor is really adding value. This is particularly true where there is a large parcel of costs that bear little resemblance to the technical expertise needed to manage those costs.

Numerous permutations on these two alternatives can be used providing they recognize the expected total profit that will result from the project.

Appendix: DCF Explanation

The basis of discounted cash flow (DCF) is that a dollar in the hand today is worth more than the promise of a dollar to be received in the future. The difference in value reflects two elements: the risk that the debtor will default and the loss of interest that could have been earned had the money been available to be invested in a riskless investment. Interest rates effectively combine both the basic cost of money plus a premium to reflect the risk of the loan.

If interest rates are presently 10%, then $100 invested today is worth $110 in one year. Similarly, $90.90 invested today is worth $100 in one year, at a 10% interest rate. The $90.90 is known as the 'present value' of $100 discounted for one year at 10%. This concept is undeniably correct and is reflected in money markets around the world.

The longer the time span of expectations, the smaller the discount factor. For example, the present value of $100 due in two years is $82.60, and in three years is only $75.10. This is not only mathematically correct, but is also logical in that the further away is the goal, the less probability there is of attaining the goal. By discounting the expectations, one can put them all on to an equal and comparable basis. These expectations can be aggregated, so that $100 to be received at the end of each of the next three years has a present value of only $248.60 ($90.90 + $82.60 + $75.10). The recipient is then indifferent to the receipt of the $100 at the end of each of the next three years or $248.60 cash in the hand today.

In DCF analysis it is fundamental to use an appropriate interest rate (or discount rate) and to understand why it applies. A *hurdle rate* is the interest rate at which a project turns from being worthwhile to not-worthwhile. The discount rate or hurdle rate has to reflect the impact of the stockholders' requirements for a reasonable return as well as the company's funding policies, including the tax implications of debt.

If the company has no debt – that is, it is funded entirely by equity – then each new project should at least make a return exactly in accordance with the stockholders' expectations. So if the stockholders expect a 17% return, new projects should be subject to a 17% hurdle rate. The company may be experiencing short-term profitability problems and only returning, say, 8% to its owners, but it does not make sense to reduce the hurdle rate down to 8%. Certainly any new project that yields more than 8% would improve the overall return. However, it may still not be enough to compete for funds in a market where a 17% return is the norm. Likewise a company currently experiencing high returns (say 25%) should not impose this abnormally high hurdle rate and so disbar projects that most other companies would be delighted to pursue.

So rather than use the company's own unique cost of equity, it should use the industry average. If the individual company then has a profusion of potential projects that pass the hurdle rate, it can optimize its results against the global average by choosing only the best of the options.

Thus investors' expectations should be calculated using a market-related rate of return, and estimation of this rate of return can be helped by using the *capital asset pricing model*. This model looks at the returns of various industrial sectors and tries to quantify the risk of that sector against the average risk for the whole market. The ratio of the industry's risk to the total market risk is termed *beta*. Published empirical results are available for various industrial sectors, as can be seen in table 6.2.

Table 6.2

Sector	Beta ratio
Air transport	1.80
Electronics	1.60
Railroads and shipping	1.20
Agriculture	1.00
Oil	0.85
Banking	0.85
Gold	0.35

The table indicates that the stock price of agricultural firms, with a beta of 1.00, has historically moved in exact correlation to the total stock market. Stock prices of the air transport firms (with a beta of 1.80) have swung more widely than the average: in boom times they have outperformed the market, and in recessions they have slumped below the average fall. Movements in the price of gold stocks, with a low beta, are measured to have had only a low correlation to the overall movement of the market.

These observations quantify the conventional logic that investors require a higher return from the more volatile stocks and so price the stock at a higher discount to its earnings potential. From these observations, the theory follows that, if the investors price the stock in this way, the company must also price its projects in the same way: thus the beta ratio is used to estimate the cost of equity for a particular industrial sector.

The *cost of equity* comprises:

- the riskless rate of return; plus
- the risk premium for venturing on to the stock market instead of choosing risk-free government bonds.

For any particular industrial sector, the risk premium is the global average risk premium multiplied by the beta ratio. For agriculture the risk premium is identical to the global average: for air transport, it is 1.8 times the global average.

If the government bond rate is 10% and the stock market rate of return is 17% then a global average 7% risk premium exists. However, for air transport the risk premium is 1.8 times 7% which is 12.6%, giving a total required rate of return of 22.6% (10% + 12.6%). This becomes the cost of equity when considering whether to buy a new aircraft.

The market rate of return presumes an average rate of risk applying to that industry, with some industries or types of company being perceived as more risky than others. The higher the perceived risk, the higher the return required by the investors. Since the risk is an average, it is unlikely to apply specifically to any individual project, and so the question arises as to whether the required rate of return should be amended to suit the riskiness of the project.

Consider a media business group that operates cinemas and makes films. The historical return to investors from the group may be 16%. However, the market rate for cinema operators may be 13%, and perhaps 30% for film makers. It would not make sense to require the cinema segment to work to a 16% hurdle rate, when its competitors are working to a 13% return: it would be outbid on proposals for new sites by competitors willing to accept a lower rate of return. Similarly, assessing film-making investments at a 16% hurdle rate would be inappropriate if competitors require a 30% return. To do so would cause a tendency to accept too many risky projects. Therefore, in a diversified business group, hurdle rates should be matched to the particular industrial sector that is being analysed.

Within the cinema segment, some sites might be more risky than others, and there is the temptation to use varying hurdle rates according to the perceived risk of the individual cinema site. Rather than manipulating the hurdle rates, 'best case', 'worst case' and 'probable case' scenarios should be calculated, all using the same hurdle rate. In effect this models the sensitivity to the business assumptions: that is, the risk of the project. This approach is more valuable than using the same data and three different hurdle rates.

So far, only the cost of equity has been discussed. The generally accepted practice is that the *weighted average cost of capital* should be used to appraise projects as this recognizes the mix of equity and debt peculiar to the investing company. Debt is significantly cheaper than equity, as tax relief is available on the interest paid. To calculate the weighted average cost of capital, it is necessary to take the cost of equity and the after-tax cost of debt and weight them according to the usual mix of equity and debt. For example:

Equity	$100m @ 17%	=	$17m
Debt	$100m @ 8% (after tax)	=	$ 8m
Total	$200m		$25m

Weighted average = ($25m/$200m) =   12.5%

In this example, the company has a cost of equity of 17% and a cost of debt of 8%. The weighted average is 12.5% and is the hurdle rate used for appraising its normal investments.

7

Helping the Sales Manager

The price of goods and services, in the long run, depends on their cost, which in this sense means both capital and operational expenditure. To this must be added some reward for the businessman or woman who takes the risk of setting up the production machinery and finding the customer. In the short term, prices may have only a loose connection with actual costs as competitors, or even customers, move the price to satisfy short-term objectives.

The term *costing* means identifying the resources used by a particular product, business segment or activity. It is vital knowledge as it will affect decisions on investment, pricing and physical management of the production and delivery processes. In the pricing context, it is possible to become needlessly scientific about costing products and services because pricing is mostly an exercise in the understanding of human behaviour, which defies the spreadsheet and the calculator. On the other hand, sometimes costs need to be known in fine detail, for example to gauge the impact of alternative ways of working. If the factory is processing ten million items each year and it is possible actually to save one cent of marginal cost on each item, then that is something worth knowing and acting upon.

Most people in business have an instinctive feeling for their costs and how those costs relate to competitors, even if they cannot precisely articulate the level of cost and the differentials. An experienced operator in a business builds up a feel for several key indicators of productivity and by looking at those indicators can quickly gauge the broad level of relative costs. It is only when cost differentials become very narrow that a cost accountant is needed to calculate costs to a fine level of detail. Herein lies the problem: costing is so heavily dependent on the underlying concepts that the fine level of detail can be false if illogical concepts are being used. So cost accountants must focus on the concepts and, once these are clear, the techniques will look after themselves.

The total bundle of income and costs of a business can be carved up in an infinite variety of ways according to the topic that is under examination. When sales managers ask for the cost of a product, they do not want four different answers, nor do they want a different answer each time they ask the same question. So the company has to develop its own consistent set of costing rules that correspond with the way the business actually functions.

In some factories labour may be considered a variable cost, while in another, almost identical factory it may be considered an indirect or overhead cost. Deciding on which costing reality will prevail is the job of the costing expert, who must then educate users of costing information as to how the rules operate and their strengths and weaknesses. Consistency of terminology is essential as a business cannot afford to have its staff talking at cross purposes to each other.

The companies that are good at costing are very likely to be good at many of the other things they do. Good costing is the result of good management, whereby a succession of penetrating questions force a good costing system to evolve. Furthermore, a good costing system can improve management practices providing the cost accountant has sufficient standing in the organization to exert influence on the decision processes.

The costing of products and activities is unlikely to provide absolute answers to many questions. However, this does not mean that a detailed cost examination should be bypassed. It is an important component of the myriad of pieces of information that are needed to make complex decisions. For example, the production manager may say, 'I realize that this machine is a high-cost alternative, but I believe the higher costs are outweighed by the production flexibility it will give us.' She has made a subjective judgement which was aided by hard facts. She could not have safely made that value judgement without knowing the relative costs of this machine against the other options. A worthwhile costing service has been provided, even if the cost accountant is annoyed that the costing analysis was ignored by the production manager in choosing the machine with the higher costs.

Costing and Cost Reduction

> Competitive pressures set the price for us and the only way for us to forge ahead is to become the most cost-efficient operator in the industry. I need a strong cost accounting function to help us to make the best decisions on cutting costs.

Cost accountants mostly become involved with productivity in the setting of standard costs or in quantifying costs and benefits for investment decisions. Cost accountants are not productivity experts and their role is limited to that of supporting the work of experienced industrial engineers. The job of the cost accountant is to translate physical measurements into dollars and cents in a logical and consistent manner, and this is a worthwhile service. But it is fallacious to think that a good costing function is synonymous with tight cost control.

Apart from translating physical measures into money values, the cost accountant can also provide a worthwhile service by being the 'librarian' of useful information. In most companies there is a host of statistical data that may some day come in useful when studying some facet of business operations. Knowing where the data is, how to access it and its reliability is a task well suited to the cost accountant.

Part of this library of data will be the physical standards used in the bookkeeping system to generate standard costs. These physical standards have to be prepared by industrial engineers; the cost accountant translates them into money terms and they are then used to value inventories and the cost of goods sold. The cost accountant has an in-depth knowledge of the assumptions that underlay these physical standards and so should be able to ensure the standards are used sensibly as part of the business decision process.

As part of the training for the cost accounting role, numerous costing techniques are taught. To a great extent, these techniques are counterproductive in that they foster the illusion that there is some correct way of 'costing'. A grasp of the broad concepts is the most essential element of the costing role: in particular, an understanding of the debate about allocation of costs and an understanding of the concept of discounted cash flow. Next comes a detailed understanding of how the business operates in real life. Once these two hurdles have been overcome, the techniques are self-evident and usually involve only simple mathematics or personal computer skills.

A healthy costing system is one in which the concepts are periodically questioned and are then capable of being defended in logical terms by the costing expert. If the costing expert has merely continued with a way of doing things established by his or her predecessor and cannot defend the principles, then it is unlikely that the costing function is equipped to assist in complex business decisions.

Cost Allocation

> There seems to be much feuding between the accountants as to whether they should use full costs or marginal costs. It is not a good advertisement for their trade if they cannot even agree on the fundamentals.

In all businesses, some costs can be clearly traced to a product: these are known as *direct costs* and represent no conceptual problems. But there is inevitably an amorphous pool of *overheads* or *indirect costs* that can only be assigned to a product by some, at best, dubious process of allocation. The dilemma is whether to bother with this allocation exercise and the answer lies solely in whether the allocation improves the decision-making process.

Cost allocation is a great temptation for the cost accountant as, at a few deft strokes of the calculator, answers can be provided to excruciatingly awkward questions, such as 'How much does it really cost us?' The notion that there exists an absolute answer is fostered by the financial accountants and regulators who believe that a set of accounts can show a true and fair view by allocating indirect costs to the inventory valuation. This notion filters into the internal management of the business because it is an intellectually easier concept to handle (that there is an absolute answer) and it provides a consistency between the external accounts and the internal accounts (that is, they are both consistently wrong).

Absorption costing, which is the technical term for the art of allocating costs, versus *marginal costing*, which is the technical term for presenting costs free of allocations, is one of the never-ending bones of contention among cost accountants. Views are entrenched and no solution is in sight. Further confusion arises when accountants talk of variable and fixed costs. A company has to establish an infrastructure to support its operations. The cost of this infrastructure is often termed a 'fixed cost', but this is not helpful. All costs have to be considered variable; the only thing in question is the time span in which the costs can vary. The only useful categorization is into *direct costs* (which are clearly traceable to the subject being reviewed) and *indirect costs* (which are everything that are not direct costs).

A brief look at the major categories of a company's costs serves to highlight which types of cost are direct costs and therefore which types are indirect (infrastructure) costs.

Raw Materials   For high-volume raw materials, usage can usually be closely correlated to the volume of output and thus can be thought of as a direct cost of the product.

Labour   The number of production hours worked can usually be correlated to the volume of output and thus can be thought of as a direct cost. The non-working time of production labour cannot usually be traced to any one product and thus is an indirect cost. Usually, the time of support personnel (e.g. purchasing, cleaning or security) is considered an indirect cost; however, some support functions can be clearly traced to a product, product group or segment of the market (e.g. the time of the export sales department staff is a direct cost of conducting export sales).

Fuel and Power   For power-intensive processes there is normally a metering system that can be used to correlate usage to output, and this indicates that fuel and power is a direct cost. The relationship can be confused where continuous production processes are used, since decreased production does not necessarily mean a proportional reduction in power costs. There is inevitably power consumption on peripheral activities that have only a loose connection with the volume of output, and these are considered to be indirect costs.

Ownership of Plant and Machinery   It is often possible to record the times machines are used on specific products or jobs. The direct costs of operating the machine are normally the maintenance costs and sometimes, if equipment wears out in proportion to its workload, the replacement cost of the equipment: such costs should be assigned to the product. Historical depreciation costs are irrelevant to any current or future decision process as these relate to the sunk cost of a historical equipment purchase decision.

Research and Development   These are either sunk costs in terms of current products or else they relate to future products. Either way they have no connection to costing current products and must be considered as indirect costs. As part of the decision to introduce or change a product, the R. & D. costs need to be estimated, but once the decision to proceed has occurred, then it serves no purpose to consider R. & D. costs as direct costs.

Sales and Marketing   Selling costs and commissions often vary according to the marketing tactics applicable to a specific product. For example, door-to-door sales have different cost implications from mail-order sales. It is vital to recognize these cost differentials when comparing the profitability and pricing tactics of the alternative ways of selling the product. Similarly, advertising and promotional costs should be ascribed to products, markets or segments wherever cost differentials are significant and can be clearly traced. Certain sales or marketing costs vary according to the product's stage in its life cycle, with new products typically incurring large launch costs. Users of the costing information have to be made aware that such distortions are occurring, otherwise they may be misled when considering short-term profitability and pricing issues. There is inevitably a considerable amount of indirect costs in the form of general image advertising that relates to the broad product range rather than to individual products.

Support Activities   In special cases, support activities, such as purchasing, warehousing and delivery, can be traced to specific products, but usually they are indirect costs.

Funding Costs   The costs of holding large inventories of finished goods are a direct function of the manufacturing or marketing tactics for a specific product. Holding inventories has a clearly traceable cost impact as it ties up money that could otherwise have been invested to earn interest. Similarly, for certain customer segments, the terms of payment (30 days, 90 days, etc.) are inextricably linked to pricing decisions. The volume of money outstanding has a direct cost in terms of interest forgone. Apart from these factors, funding costs are an indirect cost that should not be attributed to specific products.

In many businesses, the indirect costs are a much higher proportion of the total costs than are the direct costs. This is part of a trend that will continue as more automation occurs and as flexible manufacturing systems can produce an array of related products. There is a great temptation to apportion the indirect costs to products in order to satisfy the recurring query, 'How much does it cost?' Inevitably, only an arguable and arbitrary basis for apportionment can be found. For example, to apportion the factory rent to a product, it is usual firstly to apportion the rent to machines based on the floor area they occupy, then to apportion the total machine cost (which now includes rent) to the product according to the budgeted machine hours per product. At face value this appears logical; however, it is misleading in that it makes a connection between a variable production volume and an infrastructure cost that will only vary if the rent is renegotiated or the factory closed.

The absorption costing logic immediately falls over when the existing machine is replaced with a similar machine that occupies half the floor area of the previous machine. To say that the product cost has now decreased is to say that the factory is now smaller than it used to be, so incurring less rent, or that the cost of other products has suddenly increased to make up for the smaller cost absorption of the new machine. Since either argument is fallacious, the cost allocation of the factory rent has clouded the decision process rather than clarified it.

The terms direct and indirect cost are meaningful only when used in the context of a specific activity or function. For example, the time of the factory gatekeeper is a direct cost of the security function. The security function is a direct cost of operating the Eastwood Warehouse. The Eastwood Warehouse is a direct cost of the Eastern Region sales network. The Eastern Region sales network is an indirect cost when considering individual products sold in the region.

This is the type of costing reality that a company should pursue and promulgate to all its managers. Absorption costing and its spurious cost allocations must be firmly laid to rest, to reappear only as a source of amusement in the accounting history books.

Responsibility for Pricing

> Pricing is such a difficult issue that many of our salesmen try to dodge the issue by seeking some mathematical certainty from the costing clerks. We need to establish a pricing mechanism that uses facts wherever possible but which also emphasizes the wheeling and dealing ability of the salesmen.

Since costs and price have an undeniable medium-term linkage, there is a temptation to try and simplify the pricing mechanism by tying it to the costing system. In effect sales managers are then trying to delegate the difficult part of their job to cost accountants, as exemplified in the following scenario.

The cost accountant is busily calculating her monthly standard costs when the sales manager dashes into the office. He demands, 'I've got the General Sludge Corporation on the phone. They want to buy 300 tons of our Grade BB sludge. What does it cost us?' The cost accountant refers to her cost ledger and advises that it costs $120.80 per ton. The sales manager rushes back to his telephone, adds 25% normal mark-up and advises General Sludge that it will cost them $151 per ton plus delivery. General Sludge thank him very much for his prompt assistance and say they will think about it.

The sales manager is content that he has responded quickly to a potentially valuable new customer. He has been trying for several months to think of ways of moving the Grade BB sludge. The cost accountant is content that she has helped the sales manager, but she is a bit uneasy as to whether she really gave the right answer. 'Still, if I don't know the real cost, then nobody else is likely to know. I'm on fairly safe ground.' She goes back to her work of apportioning the factory rental cost across all the product line, which includes Grade BB sludge.

The cost accountant has every reason to feel uneasy. She could not say to the sales manager, 'I don't know the cost', or 'Which cost do you want?', or 'The cost is indeterminate.' Really she should have said, 'Why do you want to know the cost? Pricing? Tell them to ring back in an hour and meanwhile we'll talk about how we should set a price.'

Pricing can be one of the most complex of business decisions, involving competitive strategy and customer evaluation. It would be wonderfully simple if one only had to work out the costs, add a standard profit and issue a price list. If it was so simple, anybody could be successful in business.

Absolute answers are most unlikely when it comes to pricing decisions. Pricing should be based upon what the market will bear and hopefully, but not necessarily, the price will exceed the cost of delivering the product. If it does not, the options are to reduce costs or get out of the market. Merely to calculate the costs and add a mark-up is to try and simplify a world that is not simple. Sometimes one can get away with the simplistic mark-up approach, but the probability is that it will only lead to accidental underpricing of the product. In a competitive market, there is no chance of consistently overpricing the product: the customers will eventually force your prices down by purchasing from your competitors.

So the key exercise in costing existing products for pricing purposes is to decide whether one wants to be in the market given a certain price and how low the price can drop before one has to leave the market. These are fundamental decisions to any business and costing plays a vital role. But the point that must be hammered home to sales managers is that they set the prices; cost accountants tell them whether the business can sustain that price. Too often cost accountants are forced to do the sales managers' work for them.

Business Segmentation

> The financial controller seems to see his costing department as a tool to keep the salesmen honest. I see it as a tool to help the salesmen make the best decisions for the business, within a highly competitive market.

The costing function has to be reactive to the needs of the sales manager. Cost accountants can influence the decision-making process by the way they present information, and they have an important role in explaining costing concepts to users of this information. Their success in this area will greatly depend upon the credibility they inspire in the sales manager, and that credibility may have to be won partly by shooting down some of the more fanciful notions that are in the latter's optimistic nature.

Sales managers regularly need to know the margin on the products under their control, since by comparing costs and income they can decide on their marketing tactics. If they have a low-margin product, they are less likely to discount its price in the face of competitive pressures than if they have a high-margin product. Also, when considering product changes or the introduction of new products, sales managers need to know the direct costs so that they can assess the market's ability to absorb those costs through selling prices.

Apart from just looking at products in isolation, the sales manager has to look at individual customers or customer groupings. Sometimes it makes more sense to segment the market by customer grouping, particularly where a bundle of products or services is offered and there is cross-subsidization between products. So the first step in deciding how to present costing information is to segment the business into meaningful chunks that accord with how the product or the market is perceived and managed.

Essentially, segmentation can be by product, by customer type, by geography or according to divisions of managerial responsibility, which could be some combination of the product, the customer and geography.

In some industries, definition of 'the product' is simple – GM produces cars and Boeing produces planes. In service industries in particular, it can be more complicated. Does IBM produce computers or computer systems? Is an IBM mainframe operating system a separable product even though it generates sales and costs on its own? Does a bank have separable products or does it really only have separable customers?

The traditional definition of a product should not be taken for granted. The customer's perception of a product may well be different from the supplier's, and it is the customer perception that really matters. For example, a company sells equipment and provides after-sales service. Although the seller sees the equipment as the product, the customer sees the after-sales service as the product that it purchased. The purchaser could have bought the equipment elsewhere at a lower price, but chose this supplier to ensure smooth introduction of the new technology. In these circumstances it would be appropriate for the selling company to segment its market according to:

- leading edge sales, with a high level of sales support;
- conventional systems, with a predetermined level of sales support; and
- simple systems, with little or no sales support.

This contrasts to a segmentation based on machine type A, machine type B, etc. The leading edge segmentation allows better decisions on competitive pricing tactics as it recognizes the customer perception of value and this would hopefully accord with marketing strategies.

Initially a company may not know the best way to segment its business and this will presumably be reflected in poorly defined marketing strategies. But in rapidly evolving markets it is difficult to determine what is really happening and so some experimentation is required. If a company can successfully segment the market in a superior way to its competitors, it will gain an important strategic advantage. It can then clearly focus its efforts to satisfy a niche and, with the benefit of being first into a new market, it can protect that niche from competitors.

If sales managers have a clear perception of how they are trying to segment the market, then cost accountants must support that thrust even if it breaks with traditional views or causes headaches in trying to assemble the data. If cost accountants do not support sales managers, they will no doubt do their own back-of-the-envelope calculations and will most likely make some costly errors.

The major trap for the cost accountant is the availability of basic data. It is the soft option to prepare financial reports based upon available information rather than to gamble with approximations and surveys. The cost accountant usually considers that the best personal option is to play safe and only to deliver proven information, even if it is at odds with what is really needed. This trait follows from the proposition that costing is an accurate science and that to deliver information of dubious parentage is inconsistent with being a professional accountant.

There is nothing wrong with approximations providing the user is made aware of the margin for error. The margin for error can most easily be stated if there is some total and absolute answer that can be used as a benchmark. For example, the sales manager wants to know the cost of providing after-sales service to leading edge system sales. Therefore the cost accountant organizes a sample survey of the support engineers' timesheets and estimates that it cost $1.2 million over the last six months. To assess the reasonableness of this estimate, it has to be compared with the total cost of the support function which was $2 million. Therefore the estimate is that 60% of the costs are related to leading edge systems, and the cost accountant and sales manager can look at the 60% result and decide whether it is realistic. Without knowing what the total costs were, it would be difficult to put the estimate into perspective and see whether it made sense.

Although estimating is an inevitable part of costing, it must be informed. This means that a routine database of information is required from within which various approximations can be made and compared to known figures.

Contribution Measurement

In our business, we deal with mass markets where competitive pressures are the dominant feature of our pricing. We closely watch the competitors and ensure that we match them in terms of marketing and cost control. Our major controllable is our sales mix and I want to ensure we keep a tight control on this.

In most business situations the product manager has a portfolio of products, most of which have been inherited, and pricing has evolved through market forces and various deliberate or inadvertent circumstances. The product manager has to monitor the products, or market segments, in terms of what is happening in the market place and in terms of how it translates into overall corporate performance. Neither the external nor the internal information is of any use in isolation: they need to be combined to form a complete picture that will allow the best decision.

In terms of external pressures, market intelligence is absolutely vital. This may mean having one of the sales staff walking around the shops looking at competitors' prices, or it may entail employing market research consultants to survey customer perceptions. Where a company has direct access to the eventual customer, the sales staff can gather much useful data on the effects of marketing campaigns and pricing strategies and how these are perceived to relate to the offerings from competitors. Many companies are removed from the customer by means of wholesalers, in which case customer contact has to be made by means of surveys.

The internal information is best achieved through a *contribution report*. Contribution is the difference between the sales income and the direct costs of delivering the product. Contribution is then expressed as a percentage of the sales income, usually termed the gross margin or contribution margin, as shown in the simple example in figure 7.1. This type of report can be produced by product type or customer type, or by whatever other segmentation assists in monitoring pricing trends.

In this example, the gross margin has fallen between this year and last year but further consideration is needed before prices are

	This year	Last year
Sales income	100	90
Less: Direct costs	(70)	(60)
Contribution	30	30
Contribution margin	30%	33%

Figure 7.1   Simple Sales Corporation: contribution report ($000)

automatically raised to reinstate the previous level of profitability. It could be that last year was an exceptional year and that competitive pressures have now reduced prices to more normal levels. Or the company may have increased its cost structure. If the cost increase is likely to have hit competitors equally hard, a price increase is a possibility. But if the cost increase is unique to this company, it is unlikely that any price increases will be matched by competitors and the new set of prices will be too high, causing lower sales volumes.

The contribution report does not tell the business which alternative is the truth, but it at least indicates that something has changed and that what it is should be discovered. For the contribution report to be of use as a means of monitoring the connection between costs and prices, it must reflect current costs and it must exclude any apportioned costs.

If the contribution report reflects old costs (for example, depreciation of an asset purchased two years ago, or stock purchased six months ago), then it only clouds the ability to make decisions, although in accounting terms it may be mathematically correct. There is no reason why current pricing decisions should reflect historical windfalls or losses.

Likewise, if the costs include an apportionment of some central pool of costs, the decision process will be degraded rather than enhanced. The reason that any cost has to be apportioned is that it cannot be clearly traced to a particular product. That being so, the contribution information is being contaminated with guesses about how products should share indirect costs. There is nothing wrong with guesses providing they serve some useful purpose, but in this case, nothing extra can be added to the understanding of changes in costs that are unique to the product or market segment that is being reviewed.

In addition to helping monitor existing products, the contribution statement also provides a good indicator for price setting on new or enhanced products. The first step in pricing a new product is to estimate the direct costs of the new product. To that figure can be added the contribution that is being earned on similar products, to give a benchmark price. The actual launch price for the product can use the benchmark price, adjusted upwards or downwards according to competitive pressures, novelty value or any expected gradual decline in costs.

Cross-subsidization

> With the benefit of hindsight, it is obvious that we have been
> victims of some clever niche marketing by small competitors. They
> have targeted our high-volume customers but only over a narrow
> product range. Individually it didn't seem a problem, but collec-
> tively it has made quite a dent in our profits.

Cross-subsidization is the situation where the contribution on one
product in the business props up low contribution or losses in
other products. This can arise from the customers' perception of
good value, which governs the pricing arrangements, or through
default, in that the vendor does not realize that cross-subsidization
is happening.

Whether cross-subsidization is deliberate or not, its existence is
an important piece of information as it means that one product
must be earning super returns to make up for the shortfall on the
other products. A competitor can recognize these high returns
and target that product at more normal price levels. Failure to
recognize what is happening can lead to loss of the good product
or market segment and retention of the low-price products. This
scenario is especially true in the insurance industry, where an
insurance company can be left with all the bad risks and does not
realize it until it is too late and the claims start rolling in. Once
the good business segment is lost, it requires a large effort to
regain it.

To monitor cross-subsidization, a contribution statement
should be prepared for various products or business segments.
From this, the extent of cross-subsidization should be evident.
However, it is useful only if the business is segmented in the same
way as the competitors look at the market. By knowing the extent
of cross-subsidization, the business can organize itself either to
gradually remove the anomaly or to resist threats from niche
marketing competitors.

Figure 7.2 shows a contribution statement for an insurance
company which identifies that the pricing of sports car, motorbike
and pleasure boat business needs urgent review as this business is
being subsidized by high prices on the house contents product.

Line of business	Premium income (%)	Commissions paid (%)	Claims costs (%)	Processing costs (%)	Underwriting profit (%)	($m)
House contents	100.0	5.2	65.0	7.0	22.8	12.250
House fire risks	100.0	6.0	74.0	5.0	15.0	3,687
Cars – Sports	100.0	6.7	123.0	9.0	−38.7	(6.538)
Cars – Under 25	100.0	6.5	73.0	9.0	11.5	1.687
Cars – 26 to 40	100.0	6.6	83.0	9.0	1.4	2.393
Cars – 40+	100.0	4.3	74.0	9.0	12.7	1.253
Motorbikes	100.0	7.5	98.0	12.3	−17.8	(1.789)
Boats – Commercial	100.0	3.8	74.0	12.6	9.6	1.230
Boats – Pleasure	100.0	2.5	88.0	12.0	−2.5	(3.630)
	100.0	5.0	83.0	9.7	2.3	10.543

Figure 7.2 Quickpay Insurance Company: contribution report, previous twelve months

Relationship Pricing

> We have products but the key to our success is in targeting large customers and offering them a complete service which precludes them from ever contacting our competitors. Sure we lose money on some products, but that is a cost of cementing the customer relationship.

If the customer relationship can be tied in through some loss leaders, then that is a legitimate business tactic providing the overall result is positive. To make this assessment, it is necessary to look at all the services offered to the customer and to tally up their profits and losses. The following example of this *customer evaluation* process concerns a bank that has a large corporate customer with numerous lines of business running simultaneously.

Facility/product		Volume ($m)	Margin (%)	Profit ($m p.a.)
Overdraft facilities		225	0.950	2.138
Lending fees charged				0.180
Less: Credit risk			−0.500	(1.125)
Less: Management costs				(0.150)
Transaction processing				
Cheques paid ($m)				
Fees charged	0.390			
Processing costs	(0.890)			(0.500)
Cash deposits ($m)				
Fees charged	0.410			
Processing costs	(0.940)			(0.530)
Money market transactions		1,550	0.110	1.705
Foreign exchange turnover		2,895	0.013	0.376
Fees on overseas transactions				0.367
Less: Trading costs				(0.120)
Less: Clerical costs				(0.189)
Relationship Profit				2.152

Figure 7.3   Customer relationship pricing: customer, Big Deal Traders Inc.

Note: Credit risk has to be deducted as it is built into the pricing of loans. If omitted, it would show high-risk customers as being more profitable.

The customer has shops all over the country and uses many different branches for banking its cash. However, there is one relationship manager at the bank's head office that sets the national pricing that applies to the customer's banking activities. The evaluation is shown in figure 7.3 and indicates that the transaction processing work is losing money.

There is nothing to stop the customer from obtaining competitive quotations for the other parts of its banking needs, but the bank's relationship manager can drop heavy hints that the cheque account fees would have to increase dramatically if it lost the profitable business. This tactic would be a last resort as normally the bank's relationship manager would sell the benefits of staying with a bank that 'knows its customers and can provide the convenience of a complete service'. Whatever tactics are used, it is essential for the bank to know where it stands when negotiating with the customer.

8

The Limiting Factor

The contribution statement gives a good idea of how prices should be moved in order to keep pace with direct costs. It says nothing about how to monitor and recover indirect costs and an adequate net profit. By definition it cannot, because we have said that indirect costs and net profit do not belong to any one specific product. However, in a job costing business there has to be a mechanism for quoting prices to the customer in the knowledge that the pricing mechanism will allow the business to recover all its costs and make an adequate profit.

Pricing Jobbing Work

> We are a jobbing business and every day we have to provide competitive quotations on a host of complex jobs. We need a reliable formula that will ensure we price competitively, consistently and profitably.

Setting prices by adding an arbitrary mark-up to direct costs will probably distort the pricing structure, as the following example demonstrates. Consider a garage that is to fit a new engine to a motor car. It buys in the engine for $2,000 and then uses ten hours of labour. Another job is to respray a car and this also needs ten hours of labour but only $100 of paint. If the recovery of indirect costs and profit were based on total direct costs, then the engine replacement job would attract a proportionately far higher price than the respray job, as shown in figure 8.1.

The profit distortion is so great ($660 versus $90) for what is the same consumption of time and skill, that this garage is unlikely to win any jobs for engine replacements but is going to win all the

	Engine job	Respray job
Materials Costs	2,000	100
Labour @ $20 per hour	200	200
Direct Costs	2,200	300
Standard 30% mark-up	660	90
Selling Price	2,860	390

Figure 8.1　Pricing as a mark-up on direct costs ($)

respray jobs. Since it makes a contribution of only $90 on each respray job, and only $9 per hour worked, it will probably find that it is still not recovering enough towards its indirect costs and so cannot make a reasonable profit.

To overcome this type of distortion, one could specify that indirect costs and profit will be recovered in respect of labour hours only (say, $50 per hour), in which case the engine job would be priced at $2,700 ($2,200 + $500) and the respray job at $800 ($300 + $500). This is more likely to give a sensible pricing structure and one that compares with what competitors are doing. A business that is setting its prices like this should also routinely monitor its results on the same basis. Thus it should report the contribution per hour sold, and hopefully this will average $50 per hour.

This simple concept can be taken further by identifying the *limiting factor* that constrains production and then setting prices in relation to usage of that limiting factor. The limiting factor concept is based on the assumption that there exists a bottleneck in the production system, perhaps a specialized or high-cost machine, or a shortage of workers with a particular skill. The aim of the business should be to optimize its profits by relating the pricing of jobs to the usage of that limiting factor.

For example, a specialized engineering workshop has to produce job quotations for numerous jobs and it wants to establish a basic pricing structure. The limiting factor for the workshop is its milling machines, of which there are ten, each capable of doing 2,000 hours of work per annum. It estimates the amount of money that all the jobs will have to recover in order to make a net profit of $800,000 per annum:

	$m
Production indirect costs	2.0
Support department costs	1.0
Profit before interest and tax	0.8
Amount to be recovered from work	$3.8m p.a.

The required recovery per limiting factor is $3,800,000/20,000 hours = $190 per hour. So the job quotation system is based on:

- calculating the direct costs of doing the job;
- adding on $190 for each hour that it is expected the milling machines will be used on the job;
- amending the price upwards or downwards where necessary according to the unique requirements of the job or the customer.

The quotation for a particular job using this formula is set out in figure 8.2. There is the possibility that the milling machines may

---

Job # 1234   Customer: Deep Goldmines   Due: 5/5/_8

Job description:...............

Milling machine time: 10 hours

Direct Costs:	($)
Labour 56 hours @ $23	1,288
Materials	2,670
Transport	125
	4,083
Add: Standard margin	
10 hours @ $190	1,900
Less: Advance order discount	(183)
Quoted Selling Price	5,800

Figure 8.2   Job quotation worksheet

not be used for 20,000 hours next year because demand is less than expected. This means that the limiting factor has now ceased to be a limiting factor and the company may have to look for a new rationale for its pricing structure, probably reverting to a recovery on labour hours worked. Alternatively, it could stay with the limiting factor formula but be prepared to offer price discounts to improve volume and keep the workshop fully occupied.

Monitoring the Limiting Factor

At the top level of the business, I cannot be involved in detailed pricing decisions, but I want to know where the problem areas are and to be able to monitor progress.

Even if prices are not actually set according to the limiting factor formula, the concept is useful when monitoring the relative performance of products. The examples in figure 8.3. give an indication of how potential problem areas have been highlighted for further investigation. Having identified products with problems relative to other products, it is necessary to decide on changed prices, lower costs or curtailing that product altogether.

Figure 8.3   Examples of monitoring product pricing by reference to the limiting factor

Engineering Contractor

Business segment	Gross profit ($000)	Gross profit per machine hour ($/hr)	
Small commercial	2,000	43	
XYZ tanker contract	2,800	26	
Govt. maintenance works	5,150	86	
Middle East exports	580	73	
European exports	3,750	15	XXXXX
Other	310	26	
Total	14,590	49	

Figure 8.3 cont.

Bank

Business segment	Operating income ($000)	Return on capital (%)	
Domestic housing	5,580	11.00	
Commercial loans	7,310	12.50	
Credit cards	830	13.80	
Transaction processing	(650)	−3.50	XXXXX
Foreign exchange	510	23.00	
Money market trading	220	4.00	XXXXX
	13,800	9.75	
Deposit taking	6,350	N/A	
Income Before Indirect Costs	20,150	14.24	

Retailer

Business segment	Operating income ($000)	Income per sq. metre ($ p.a.)	
Food – Vegetables	1,100	27	XXXXX
Food – Meat	1,500	56	
Food – Groceries	4,600	54	
Food – Specialities	800	65	
Clothes – Fashion	2,300	70	
Clothes – Children's	1,800	49	
Hardware	900	32	
Electrical appliances	3,300	68	
Income Before Indirect Costs	16,300	52	

Note: Operating income is after charging sales staff costs.

For example, the retailer shown in figure 8.3 has a variety of product lines: some, such as food, have low margins but a high turnover; others, such as fashion clothes, have high margins but a low turnover. The retailer has a limited floor space (his limiting factor) and it is his intention to optimize his contribution per square metre. If he can make $70 per square metre per annum from fashion clothes and $55 per square metre per annum from food, then he has a good indicator of the relative worth of his product lines. He is also told that he is averaging $52 per square metre per annum overall, resulting in an operating profit of $16.3 million, which is considered by the board of directors to be inadequate in comparison to the capital investment.

This information is only the start of the decision-making process for the retailer. Some of his floor space is only appropriate to food and some would be wasted on anything except high fashion. He has to juggle his constraints to optimize the total return. Having optimized his allocation of floor space between food and clothes, his next task is to look at individual food products and see if any are causing a problem. He then finds that vegetables are making only 50% of the returns that can be obtained from confectionery. So he reduces the vegetables sales area and increases vegetable prices. He uses the free space for more confectionery displays. It is a never-ending juggling act between prices, the scarce resource and the selling volumes. The juggling act is bound to be more rational if it is supported with financial information pertinent to the problems facing the retailer.

Pricing for Risk

> When we tender for a job we try to minimize the risks by good research. However, there must always remain an element of risk and I want that quantified so that we know what we may be letting ourselves in for.

An essential element in any business is risk. Business is confronted with risks of all kinds and they need to be factored into pricing decisions in a logical manner. Broadly speaking, they can be categorized as:

- *operational risk*, which is the chance that the technology could go wrong;
- *customer risk*, which is the chance that the customer could default on his or her payments;
- *financial risk*, which is the chance that interest rates, exchange rates or commodity prices could move in the wrong direction;
- *market risk*, which is the chance that a competitor could come up with a superior product or engage in price discounting to win

market share, or that there may be some other radical change in the market.

Some of these risks can be hedged or minimized. For example, operational risk could be minimized by sticking to proven technology; customer risk could be minimized by seeking bank guarantees of payment or by extensive credit checks; financial risk could be eliminated by forward purchase of currency or commodities, or by using fixed-rate funding; market risk can sometimes be contained by forward selling a product, although there is not much that can be legally done about the threat from competitors, except to have good competitor intelligence.

The impact of business risk needs to be taken into account in costing and pricing exercises; if not in money terms, then at least in the form of a statement that acknowledges the risk and its probability of occurrence. To demonstrate how risk can be built into a benchmark price, an extended example follows concerning the preparation of a tender for a civil engineering contract. As a by-product, this example observes that internal service departments must be priced at market rates or else they confuse the assessment of risks and price negotiations.

The Saturn Contracting Company is putting in a tender for an irrigation control station that will drain low-lying land prior to a major housing development. The company is organized so that it has a pool of resources that it allots to contracts as they occur. These resources comprise project managers, technicians, labour, plant and computers. For example, the company has a fleet of dump trucks available for use in the engineering contracts.

Within the company there has been much debate as to whether the accounting cost of trucks should be factored into contract prices or whether market rates should be used. Because many of the trucks are quite old, the accounting cost is computed to be $200 per day, but comparable trucks have to be hired at a market rate of $350 per day from a plant hire company. Naturally the engineers want to price the trucks at $200 per day as this gives more chance of winning the contract. The financial controller argues that, if a specialist plant hire company needs $350 per day to make the trucks worthwhile, then it is highly unlikely that a non-specialist is going to be able to do the same function for nearly half the price. Anyway, he argues, if we do have a windfall on these trucks, why should it be given away to the customer? Furthermore, sometimes there are not enough trucks and then they have to be hired for $350, yet only $200 might be allowed for in the tender price.

The financial controller's arguments are accepted and the resources available are considered as profit centres that have to recover their costs by recharges to the projects that consume those resources. These recharges for resources are valued in two different ways. For resources that are unique to the company and have no external market equivalent, they are valued at their direct cost. This applies to the time of the engineers, the technicians and the computer section. For resources that can be freely obtained on the market, market rates are used in the tender price as it makes the company indifferent to whether it owns or rents the dump trucks and other equipment.

This is as it should be, since the dump trucks are not an integral part of the business. The ownership of the dump trucks has to stand alone as a separately justified business investment, and problems or windfalls in this peripheral business activity should not interfere with the pricing of a contract that has to compete with other contractors that may or may not be pricing their dump trucks at market rates. If any price discounting has to occur at a later stage of the pricing process, at least that discounting will be done in respect of the engineering contract and not in respect of dump truck operating.

To support the tender process, the financial controller provides a schedule of resource charge-out rates to the experts preparing the tender. These rates are applied to the estimated hours needed to do the job. Where materials already in stock are to be used, these materials are valued at their replacement value even if this differs from their original cost.

In preparing a tender document, numerous technical people become involved. The danger is that these people all add a safety margin into their estimates, and that people further up the organization may not realize it and may add even more safety margin. The result can be an unnecessarily conservative estimate that fails to win the contract. The converse can also happen, resulting in the signing of a contract with only downside risk and no upside opportunity. Therefore all cost estimates contain a best case, expected case and worst case scenario, and this effectively quantifies the operational risk that is thought to exist in the project.

The customer risk is then evaluated. In this instance the customer is a highly geared property developer engaged in a speculative venture. To cover this risk, it is decided that a bank guarantee has to be available for all outstanding progress payments and that weekly progress payments will have to apply.

The financial risks are also considered, the main risk being that $1 million of electronic equipment will have to be imported from Germany and that exchange rates could fluctuate. Therefore the contract specifies an exchange rate applicable to the contract, with a time limit for contract acceptance. If the tender is successful then a forward purchase of German currency will immediately be effected. Since it is a fixed-price contract, there is no market risk to worry about.

Having assembled all the expected costs of the contract and quantified the risks, the next step is to decide on what margin is appropriate. The margin will reflect a recovery of indirect costs plus a profit element and is calculated in proportion to the limiting factor applicable to the business, as follows:

1 The company has 100 project engineers who each have 1,500 hours per annum of productive time.
2 The company has $15 million per annum of infrastructure costs that it must recover from engineering contracts.
3 The directors expect a profit from engineering contracts of $30 million this year, having considered the buoyant market conditions and the company's recent investment in increased capacity.
4 Therefore 150,000 hours of engineers' time will have to recover a total of $45 million in contribution from contracts.
5 Therefore each hour an engineer spends on a project will have to recover $300 over and above the engineer's own salary.
6 This contract requires 3,000 hours of engineers' time and so a $900,000 margin above direct cost is required.

The workings of the tender price are shown in figure 8.4. So far it is all mathematics, which is not too hard. Next comes the difficult bit: deciding at what price to pitch the tender. Here, the accountants bow out and the wily businessman takes over. His first step is to look at the operational risk. It has a downside risk of $1.41 million ($11.8 million versus $13.21 million) and a possibility of saving $1.05 million ($11.8 million versus $10.75 million). The businessman decides that he can minimize the downside risk by putting one of his best engineers in to manage the contract. He then looks at the competitors and the state of the market to gauge whether any significant discounting would be necessary. After that, he sounds out the customer to see if he already has a percep-

	Best case	Expected case	Worst case
Site clearance	0.30	0.35	0.40
Foundations	0.90	1.20	1.40
Walls and roof	1.80	1.95	2.30
Plumbing	0.35	0.45	0.60
Electricals	3.85	4.10	4.20
Project management	0.10	0.15	0.16
Fitout and commissioning	2.30	2.45	3.00
Engineering costs	9.60	10.65	12.06
Foreign exchange hedge	0.05	0.05	0.05
Payment security bond	0.20	0.20	0.20
Total cost	9.85	10.90	12.31
Standard Margin	0.90	0.90	0.90
Possible Tender Prices	10.75	11.80	13.21

Figure 8.4   Saturn Contracting Company: job quotation worksheet ($m)

tion on price. Then he tries to frame a tender that offers a price but tries to leave the door open to negotiation without loss of face. Perhaps he can say, 'The tender price is subject to a soil engineer's report', which gives him leeway to wriggle on price if necessary. But at least when he wriggles, he does so in the full knowledge of the bare facts, free of any arbitrary appointments. After plenty of objective and subjective estimates, he puts in a tender price of $12.1 million, reflecting a slightly negative bias towards the worst case.

In many construction and engineering jobs, the operational risk can be minimized by using *rise and fall contracts*. This means that the contract has certain assumptions about the cost of materials or the degree of difficulty of the job. If the costs or difficulty vary from that specified in the contract, then the contractor can pass the extra costs on to the customer. This makes life easier for the contractor as it minimizes the risk. The risk still exists, but it is borne by the customer. In such instances, there is less need to prepare the best case–worst case scenario used in the above example.

Quantity Discounts

> Give me a firm order for 50,000 door handles, and I'll offer the best price in the world. I wouldn't even bother to respond to a 5,000 item enquiry: the price I would have to quote would embarrass me.

For high-volume manufacturing to be competitive in price and quality, there has to be a relatively large investment in infrastructure costs, and the direct cost of producing one extra item will be quite small. To justify this large investment in machinery that may be severely limited in what it can be used for, the business will be willing to pay a premium (in the form of price discounts) for certainty of using the equipment at full capacity. In addition to the need for certainty of future orders, the complex machinery may need considerable set-up time to be able to operate at its maximum efficiency. This factor means that pricing will be hugely affected by the volumes that can be processed between retooling: that is, the batch size.

The following example demonstrates the cost differentials arising between short and long production runs. Consider a business

	Order size 30,000	Order size 100,000
Direct Costs		
Making moulds and dies	10,800	10,800
Set-up time 20 hours	20 hours	
Run time 150 hours	495 hours	
	170 hours	515 hours
@ $120 per hour	20,400	61,800
Materials	26,000	85,800
Total Cost	57,200	158,400
Per-Unit Cost	1.907	1.584
Cost Differential	20%	

Figure 8.5 Quantity discount calculation ($)

that has to price the same product for batch sizes of 30,000 and 100,000. The per-unit cost calculations are detailed in figure 8.5 which shows that, in this example, the smaller batch costs 20% more per unit than the large batch. The factory will have to reflect this in its pricing: even if the eventual price differential is not 20% (it could be higher or lower for strategic or other reasons), a significant differential is necessary in order to match competitors and to signal to customers that it is worth their while to aggregate small orders into large orders.

The increased cost impact of small orders is likely to be amplified by the need to have more skilled labour in the factory to retool the equipment and because short production runs allow less learning curve time to perfect any one product. The continual push towards flexible manufacturing systems is in response to the need to minimize set-up costs, which in turn allows for shorter product life cycles and more marketing opportunities.

Spare Parts Volumes

> We don't make much money on the original equipment we sell, but the margins on the spare parts are what keep our head above water. But it is difficult to decide what investment to make in spares as it has a long payback.

A variation on the components theme is where an equipment supplier has to decide on the volume of spare parts it should manufacture before breaking up the production machinery. The decision revolves around the expected selling price of the spares, the timing of when they will be sold and the cost of holding the stock for several years. Equipment manufacturers are continually faced with this type of decision and so it makes sense to devise a formula or financial model that can be repeatedly used to give a standard answer based on various assumptions.

The assumptions that are required are:

- the probable selling price, in present-day prices;
- the expected volume to be sold;
- the timing of the sales;
- the marginal cost of producing a batch of spare parts given that the equipment is already set up and does not need retooling;
- the company's cost of capital, which will reflect the interest cost of holding the goods in stock for several years.

The time lag between cash outlay and cash recovery through sales will be several years, and this requires a discounted cash flow analysis model that relates all the variables and compares the result to a target rate of return. Various assumptions on price and volume and timing can be used, with the intention of deciding what should be the optimum volume to be manufactured before the machinery is retooled for the next product.

For instance, a company manufactures pumps and has 10,000 units of the type D pump in the market. These pumps will probably survive for ten years on average and will require a new set of gears every two years. Thus 40,000 sets of gears will be needed, with sales spread over eight years. The customer would be prepared to pay $100 for each set of gears but a 50% discount will have to be given to the retailer. At a price higher than $100, the customer would probably buy a new unit. This indicates a $2 million wholesale market for these spare parts. However, since the income will trickle in over a period of eight years, the income is discounted to present values, which in this example is, say, $1.1 million. This is then expressed as a ratio of the marginal cost of manufacturing the stock, $800,000, giving a ratio of 1.38.

The company has, by a detailed study on its spare parts operations, decided that a minimum ratio of 1.7 must apply for all spare parts investments, and this current proposal does not meet that guideline. Therefore there is a decision to manufacture only 25,000 sets of gears. Having made this decision, the next decision will occur in several years when the stock starts running down to critical levels. This has to be monitored by comparing projections of future demand against current stocks. Before the stock runs out, there will have to be a decision on whether to make another batch and the original decision process will be repeated, only the marginal cost of the gears will now be much higher as production machinery will have to be retooled to make the extra stock.

Pricing will depend on what the market will bear (or on whether the company feels an obligation to support its older products) rather than on the historical sunk cost of the investment several years ago. In these circumstances, a contribution report on spare parts sales, which compares current prices to a historical investment, is of no interest as it cannot affect any operational business decision.

Research and Development Costs

For our size of business it is just too risky to speculate spending large amounts of money in research and development. We are better off paying licensing fees to the big boys who can afford the enormous costs. Unfortunately this dooms us to always being a second league player.

All businesses, to a greater or lesser extent, have to invest some of their cash flow in research on new ideas and then develop them into marketable, low-cost products. There is also the continuing need to update existing products, to meet changed customer demands, to match the competition or to reduce production costs. Without this type of investment, the company would gradually decline and eventually expire.

The relative level of investment in research and development varies greatly from one industry to another. Even in mature technologies, the investment has to continue to meet competitive pressures, and each improvement or cost reduction initiative becomes harder won and more expensive. In new technologies, there is inevitable wastage as there are so many different paths that can be taken, some of which will be dead-ends.

Research and development is one area of business where big companies have a major advantage in that they need to spend a lower proportion of their cash flow to keep ahead of their smaller competitors. The pharmaceutical companies are the obvious example of where research and development costs dominate business strategies. The company builds up a huge store of experience and sometimes a new product is discovered at a relatively low cost, but in other cases many millions of dollars are required to achieve only a minor advance. Then there has to be a large investment in testing before the drug can be released.

The question is, what is the nexus between the research and development costs and the eventual selling price? There has to be a broad connection in that the company has to generate sufficient cash flow from current operations to fund its future products. But apart from this broad connection, product pricing has to be independent of historical sunk costs. If each product had to recover only its own research and development costs, then what would happen to the costs incurred on all the fruitless projects, and why should not the benefit of years of accumulated knowledge be built into a product's price?

So from a pricing perspective, the considerations should centre on the strategic issue of competitive pricing to attract or retain market share while maintaining cash flow to fund further research and development. Competitors in the industry are faced with the same considerations and are unlikely to reduce prices dramatically and constrain their own ability to invest in further research and development. The pharmaceutical companies have an additional consideration in that the pricing of their products can be a highly emotive issue and, when looked at in isolation and measured on a marginal cost basis, some of the gross margins on their drugs appear excessive. Therefore the pharmaceutical companies have to consider public opinion when setting their prices, especially when they own sole rights to an important drug. Historical research and development costs may be used when justifying prices to a sceptical public, but in substance there cannot be a direct connection between selling prices and research and development costs for any individual product.

Costing Networks

> We have invested millions in establishing a nationwide computer bookings service. Now the challenge is to fill it to capacity, and the only pricing consideration is that of what the customer perceives as being 'good value'.

Networks imply large infrastructure costs with negligible marginal costs of adding a small increase in volume. On the other hand, large increases in volume may require a massive increase in investment. In this climate, pricing has almost nothing to do with costing: pricing is a science based on human behaviour and optimizing traffic flow. But it is worth discussing the costing implications, if only to prevent accountants from attempting a detailed and highly scientific cost exercise which will have no value.

Everyday networks are exemplified by the airline, railway and telephone systems. In all these industries there are blatant examples of pricing that is at odds with patterns of cost. For example, in the one aircraft journey there co-exist:

First-Class Passengers   Ticket price: $2,000. The traveller receives luxurious seating and unlimited champagne.

Business-Class Passengers Ticket price: $1,500. The traveller receives comfortable seating but only limited champagne.

Economy-Class Passengers Ticket price: $1,000. The traveller receives cramped seating and several cups of coffee.

Tourist-Class Passengers Ticket price is unknown since it is part of a holiday package, but it is probably about $500. The tourist receives the same service as the economy-class passenger but cannot get a refund if he or she fails to show up for the flight. The tourist must book one month in advance.

Clearly the conveyance of a first-class passenger does not cost the airline four times as much as that of a tourist-class passenger. The pricing difference is centred on the prestige and comfort of travelling first class (a reflection of human behaviour) and the ability to predict passenger volume and use spare capacity (the attempt to optimize traffic flow). An accountant might say that the pricing is irrational in that a first-class passenger probably only costs the airline 10% more than an economy-class passenger, and the pricing should reflect this. But the pricing is not irrational: it works. Through trial and error the airline companies have developed a pricing structure that allows them to optimize the income potential of the aircraft.

Another feature is evident on railways, where a ticket purchased outside of the commuter rush hours attracts a discount. The reduced price of this off-peak ticket probably contradicts the marginal cost of conducting the off-peak services where trains are run with few passengers: 90% of the traffic flows during the rush hours, and outside of these times even full-paying passengers would not cover the cost of fuel for running the trains. The purpose of the discount is to encourage passengers to avoid the peak periods and so delay the need to make large investment in an infrastructure that is only used for four hours per day. This is an example of an incentive pricing scheme that is not related to current operating costs.

Deterrent pricing is evident in the telephone systems, where prices are set on distance and time. The marginal cost of a long-distance call is negligible, but there has to be some means of preventing customers from saturating the network, which would lead to more infrastructure investment. Furthermore, most customers perceive that a long-distance call is of more value to them than a local call and are prepared to pay a higher price.

Because telephone users have this ingrained perception of value, they are not motivated to question the price differentials that arise on telephone charges based on distance.

A more subtle example of deterrent pricing can be seen where two banks agree to share their automatic teller machine (ATM) networks. Both banks have the same number of ATMs at the outset and there has to be a restraint to stop one bank increasing its customer volume but not proportionately increasing its own ATM investment, thereby saturating the other bank's network. This restraint is effected by instituting a hefty interchange fee which Bank A has to pay Bank B if its customer uses the other bank's ATM, and vice versa. The fee, say $1 per transaction, has no relationship to costs; it is merely a mechanism to ensure that both banks have an incentive to match their ATM network size to the demands of their own customers.

Accountants may be called in to assist in the cost justification of the expansion or contraction of a network. This was particularly evident when rail passenger traffic declined on branch lines as a consequence of the increased popularity of motor cars. When looked at in isolation, one branch of the network may appear to be running at a deficit. The simplistic solution is to close that branch line. The problem is, how many more passengers using other parts of the network will now abandon the network, by buying cars, because the network no longer provides a complete service? No doubt quite a few will do so, which will call into question some other branch on the network. So that next branch will be closed, further escalating the abandonment of the network. Eventually the whole network will cease to be viable but it will be too late to resurrect the closed branches. Even if the land were still available, the customers would already have bought cars and would not go back to using trains. This is an example of marginal costing providing the wrong answer and gradually eroding a network.

The same logic works in reverse with a new network, such as satellite communications. The success of the network has a compounding effect, but it requires much courage to establish the network in the first place and to see it through its initial years when it will run at a large deficit.

With networks, it seems that cost accounting has to step aside and leave the decisions to intuition and acts of faith by entrepreneurs and politicians.

Subcontracting Decisions

> As part of our drive to reduce costs and optimize our investment in plant, I have initiated a thorough review of many categories of components to see whether it is better to make them ourselves or to subcontract the work. The initial answers that I have received seem mathematically correct but intuitively wrong.

A difficult decision arises where there is a choice between making a component in-house or buying it in from an outside contractor. To assist the decision, it is tempting to calculate a full cost of in-house production so that it is easily comparable to the contractor's price, which obviously includes a recovery of the contractor's indirect costs and profit. Even so, the temptation to apportion indirect costs should be resisted as a more rational decision can be obtained without apportionments.

The circumstances surrounding the decision may be that the company is at full capacity and has to make a decision between expansion of production facilities or subcontracting the work. This is essentially a simple investment decision in which the incremental investment cost can be compared to the incremental cost of subcontracting.

On the other hand, the company may not be at full capacity, in which case the direct cost of doing the work in-house can be quite rightly compared to the full cost of the subcontractor. Even if the subcontractor is far more efficient and offers a very low price, it would not be worthwhile accepting that low price unless it is less than the in-house direct cost. While this makes sense in short-term cash flow terms, in economic terms it means that inefficient industries with sunk costs in plant and equipment will not be tempted to use efficient subcontractors. However, this will usually be only a short-term situation, as the in-house manufacturer will gradually see the return on investment fall as the cheap sub-contractors influence the market. The manufacturer will then start to look for ways of upgrading efficiency or else release some of the uneconomic spare capacity.

Allocations of indirect cost or profit attribution were not required to solve the above problem. In fact, cost allocations would only have clouded the issue and resulted in the wrong short-term decision. They might (or might not) have given a better economic decision, but in business each analysis should look at the harsh realities of that particular job or function. The strategic decisions should be kept at a higher level and not confused with micro cost–benefit exercises.

It could well be that the line of thought of the chief executive owning spare capacity is 'We have all this spare capacity and therefore it nearly always requires less cash outlay for us to make it ourselves than to buy it in ready-made. Eventually we are going to have to admit that we cannot properly compete on these components and the capacity should be closed down or used for higher-value-added goods. We need to keep a close watch on this and be prepared to pull the plug, but only when a suitable alternative arises. Until that time, it is best for us to keep using our spare capacity.'

Working to a Price

I want our managers to always be on the lookout for market opportunities. They have to be able to look at a product from the customer's perspective and then work backwards to see if we could deliver a profitable product.

Quite often products have to be designed to fit into a specific price range and it is necessary to work backwards from the selling price to see what level of costs are permissible. For example, a business-

Retail price	25.00
Less: Tax	(2.10)
Retailer's margin	(8.00)
Wholesaler's margin	(2.40)
Available Income	12.50
Normal gross margin (36%)	(4.50)
Available for Direct Costs	8.00
Packing and delivery	(0.50)
Warranty costs	(0.48)
Flex, plug and element	(2.89)
Assembly labour	(1.84)
Available for Kettle Costs	2.29

Figure 8.6   Low-price kettle calculation ($)

man feels that if he can retail an electric kettle for $25 then he will have a competitive product. The calculations for this exercise are shown in figure 8.6. In this example, the decision has come back to whether it is possible to find a supplier who can provide a basic kettle for $2.29 or less that meets certain technical standards. This in turn raises the question of what volume of production is likely, as this will heavily influence the supplier's price.

The calculation required a major assumption that a 36% gross margin would apply to this product. There is some leeway in this assumption, but in this example the business considers that this sort of margin is needed on average to cover indirect costs and profits.

Costing Complexity

> The salesmen keep coming up with all sorts of bells and whistles for our products that don't cost much and will enhance the product's image or broaden its appeal. My big worry is that these bells and whistles will make our production line so complex that we will suffer major cost increases and management problems.

Another scenario in which costing can assist pricing is where a variation on a standard product is required. A decision has to be made on the additional price, if any, that should be attached to the variation. For example, a company makes a range of products in only one colour and it is considering offering alternative colours. To assess whether this is a viable option it has to estimate the increased production costs of disrupting the production line, then gauge whether consumers are likely to pay at least the incremental costs of the changed production schedules. If it is thought that they will not pay for the cost of the extra production inconvenience, then it is necessary to estimate the loss of sales volume that may occur from having no colour options.

Superficially, the per-unit cost of the product may have only a minute change, as the cost of one type of paint is nearly identical to that of another. But in this instance the cost of disrupting the production line to accommodate different colours, plus the extra stockholding implications, is quite significant. When these costs are spread over a small volume of coloured products, the required increase in price appears to be more than the customer is likely to want to pay. Armed with this information, the sales manager is better able to decide how to tackle the problem.

9

A Framework for Control

Businesses are faced with continual decisions relating to pricing, investment and cost reduction. While these decisions can usually be supported by *ad hoc* financial studies, there also needs to be a routine reporting system in which to set the context for the micro decisions. The routine reporting system has to display the health of the business through a description of its financial structure. So it must try to say what is good or bad and to show where the business is earning income or incurring costs. Additionally, the routine reporting system provides a medium to measure how individual managers are performing. In a small business the manager can manage by walking around: that is, can exert control by constant interaction with subordinates. The manager knows what they are doing and they know what the manager wants. As the business grows in size, this intimate style of management becomes impractical and a formal control process is needed. The accounting system provides a platform for that control process providing it is used sensibly and within its limitations.

It is useful for the business activity to be reduced to financial results because money is a simple and well-understood common denominator, and it also provides a focus on the relative importance of the item in question. But income, cost or profit is an end result and the underlying cause can sometimes be better explained statistically. Therefore the control system needs to use both statistical and financial measures, with the main emphasis being on the financial effect of a manager's actions. Financial or statistical reporting systems are useless without supporting comments, primarily to explain the reasons for the results, but also to prove that a manager understands the business and has it under control.

Measuring Accountability

> Since taking over the top job last year, I have been frustrated. I pull
> the levers to try and make things happen, but I don't know if the
> levers are connected to anything.

Especially in large organizations, delegation of managerial
responsibility is preferable to heavy centralized controls. For delegation to work successfully, there has to be a mechanism that
monitors the performance of the people who have had responsibility delegated to them. Financial reporting systems are often seen
to be the ideal mechanism to monitor accountability, but this relies
on the ability of business activities to be reduced to simple money
terms and of the accountant to design reports that reflect the
actions controlled by a specific manager. Seldom are either of these
reliances well founded: accountability through accounting systems
is more apparent than real and much effort can be misdirected in
the pursuit of sophisticated financial accountability systems.

Typically, the actual amount of delegated authority in a company is imprecise even if there are attempts to define it in job
descriptions and procedures manuals. There are always differing
levels of delegation for equivalent managers based on their
perceived experience, and there are always unexpected decisions
that need urgent consideration and are not specified in the job
description. Even where there is a clear specification of who
should actually sign the bit of paper, decisions are often arrived at
through a complex process of consultation and consensus. Matrix
reporting structures further confuse the ability to define 'accountability'. Although the buck has to stop somewhere, it is not always
a simple case of deciding where that place is, except at the top
levels of the organization. So when establishing a financial
responsibility reporting system, large assumptions and compro-
mises have to be made about managers' accountabilities. There
then has to be flexibility when pinpointing the owner of a particular result.

Providing one is prepared to accept that exact accountability is
unlikely to be achieved, the formal responsibility reporting system
has a useful role. The key to the whole process is how the system is
used: that is, whether bureaucratically or sensibly.

Managing Change

> The first thing we did when we took over the Nuts and Bolts Corporation was to install a tight management reporting system to find out exactly what was going on. This caused a lot of resentment from the older managers who felt we were limiting their ability to manage. We didn't sell the change properly.

The impact of change in control systems should not be underestimated as it can alter a manager's role to a large extent. The effect is most marked where there is a considerable tightening of reporting procedures, particularly following business mergers or the upgrading of older informal control systems. By having the reporting procedures tightened, managers could easily assume that their superiors want to intrude more into day-to-day affairs by receiving better and more prompt information. In fact the real intention may be the exact opposite: to manage on a looser rein, providing there is an adequate control mechanism.

The operation of a sound reporting system forces managers to manage, in that each month they have to explain their results and in doing so take on a managerial role instead of a hands-on operational role. This can be traumatic for managers who have not been formally trained in the 'art' of management. Suddenly they are being asked to leave the comfort of immersion in technical detail and instead to pay more attention to the bureaucracy of being a manager.

Upgrading or tightening the management reporting system is often a chicken and egg conundrum. On one hand, there is no point in designing a system that perpetuates existing poor management practices, and therefore the new control system should assume that better practices will prevail once the system is introduced. On the other hand, perhaps the design should wait until management practices have improved, so avoiding having to predict the management style that may be adopted. The only practical option is to design the system to cater for good management practices, although this can provoke the reaction, 'The accountants are trying to tell me how I should run my department.'

The main factor that will improve acceptance of control systems changes is a clear and truthful explanation of the concepts underlying the system, such that managers can understand how the reports will be used by their superiors. Then the system requires tangible support from senior managers, both in the design stage and thereafter, using the system as intended and asking searching questions to reinforce the perceived importance of the system.

The management reporting system in a business will inevitably end up reflecting the management style of the senior executives. They set the standards that others will follow and it is the senior executives who have to take the ultimate responsibility for the success or otherwise of the reporting system: they cannot delegate it all to the accountants.

Transfer Pricing

We have two warring factions in the finance department. One faction wants to apportion all the central costs while the other insists this is misleading. Does it really matter?

The issue of apportioning costs can be segregated into two connected but different issues, those of *transfer pricing* and *cost allocation*. Transfer pricing is discussed first.

The need for transfer pricing stems from the desire to measure where 'value is being added' in the business process. Transfer pricing is the term given to the setting of prices for the transfer or sale of goods or services between departments of a business. It is usually a highly contentious issue because it affects the relative profit contribution of various business units and so reflects on the perceived ability of the relevant managers, with managers of profitable business units being thought to be superior to those who are managing less profitable units.

Only in the most simple of businesses can one readily say which part of the business contributes an absolute amount to the total result. In most businesses, hopefully the whole business is tightly inter-connected, leading to much reliance by one department on the success of another. In the attempt arbitrarily to separate the success of one department from that of another, internal competition and rivalry is bound to occur. In some cases this can be healthy, but it is more likely to be destructive, causing divisiveness where co-operation is needed. Any spare aggression should be reserved for external competitors.

In addition to the bookkeeping workload, a transfer pricing system is costly in terms of the managerial time spent when the inevitable disputes arise. Rather than say that transfer pricing is bad and should not be done, the rule has to be that it is only used where it is likely to lead to a better business decision. This does not solve the difficulties that will continue to reoccur with transfer pricing, but it does set a basic system design criterion that can be applied consistently.

Apart from tax schemes, transfer pricing is valid only where there is a service department that provides a discretionary service to another department: the purpose of the pricing system is to match demand for services with the user's perception of price and utility. If the goods or services were free of charge, the user would not feel constrained to demand high volumes or a high quality from the provider department. As a result, the supplier would over-service by feeling obliged to satisfy its customers' demands regardless of cost: it could not or would not tell its customer to use less of its services.

A further proviso for transfer pricing is that the user should have the possibility of going outside the organization to purchase the same service. It does not mean that the user should necessarily be able suddenly to abandon using a service department, as this would lead to short-term wastage through under-used infrastructure in the service department. But there must be the capability of alternative sources of supply. If there is no possibility of using an outside contractor, the transfer pricing mechanism can immediately be seen to be an artificial device, lacking commercial reality.

Having decided to charge for the transfer of the goods or services, the next step is to decide on the price. Only two worthwhile possibilities exist and their application depends on the circumstances. In most cases, an arm's length commercial price should be used, even if based on a broad approximation. If it is impossible to come up with even a broad approximation of a market price, this is a fair indicator that it is not a service capable of external purchase. The market price is appropriate where there is a routine supply of goods or services. However, where there is a non-routine request, a marginal cost is more relevant. For example, there is a central computer department and there is no discretion to use its services, therefore its costs are not recharged. The sales department wants a special computer report programmed. The economic cost of this small piece of work is its marginal cost – that is, the price of a computer contractor for two weeks – and this is the amount that should be recharged. It has no implications for the infrastructure cost of the main computer installation.

There can be a case for instituting transfer pricing to act as a positive deterrent to undesirable practices, particularly in the usage of computer systems. It is not possible to conjure up a market price for running a job on a computer; nor is the marginal cost relevant – either it is minute (the cost of a few pulses of electricity) or else it is massive (the cost of expanding the computer system). The purpose of the pricing structure might be to persuade users to run their computing jobs overnight instead of during the day, yet to allow some leeway for daytime jobs. This can be achieved by having a surcharge for daytime jobs. The price need not have any logical accounting base, so long as it has the desired effect of moving the workload.

In addition to constraining a user from uneconomic usage of discretionary resources, transfer pricing can act as a measure for the service department to evaluate its cost structure against a market price for its output. Many large businesses have inherited numerous service departments that they would be better off without. There is a tendency for such departments to be inefficient in that they are being managed by people who do not have the specialist experience that would allow them to survive in the external competitive market. Examples could be in-house printing, motor pool, building administration and equipment maintenance functions. These functions could be subcontracted out to specialists; even if this does not provide a significant cost reduction, at least it allows the business to focus on its area of competitive advantage and not become diverted on side issues.

The first step in controlling peripheral service departments is to put them on a commercial footing with their own contribution statement, so giving them the chance to be objectively measured. The in-house support department should have an inherent competitive advantage over subcontractors by having an intimate knowledge of their customers' needs. If the in-house service department offers a genuine lowest-cost service, it need not fear having to compete with external subcontractors.

Cost Allocation

> Before I closed the design shop I was told that it cost $500,000 a year to run. Now I am told we are only saving $300,000 a year – the other $200,000 was a cost allocation from some other department that is still spending money.

The other related issue is that of cost allocation, where there is a desire to allocate costs to various users or departments for the purpose of improved accountability and therefore improved cost control. Central to this debate is the definition of direct and indirect costs.

Direct costs are, by definition, those costs that can be clearly traced to an activity and, as such, are easily dealt with. Indirect costs (overheads) are more difficult to handle and there is frequently the temptation to pretend they are direct costs and to allocate them to activities on some quasi-scientific basis. In manufacturing industries, cost allocation is usually imposed by the need to value stock at its full cost (absorption cost), which includes an allocation of indirect costs. This style of accounting has crept into other reporting systems, sometimes needlessly.

Cost allocation is also an attempt to give a simple answer to questions of how much things cost. While accountants may understand that there are a variety of answers to how much things cost, they feel constrained to give a straight answer to a straight question, and often the answer makes more sense if they give a full cost that includes allocated overheads. When business managers ask, 'How much does our dispatch function cost?', they do not want to become involved in a philosophical debate about direct or indirect costs; they just want to know the answer. However, depending on the decision they have to make, they could be seriously misled by the answer unless they are told that it includes a large allocation of indirect costs.

There are various dubious arguments raised in support of allocating costs. One is that the line divisions need to be made aware of the level of group overheads they have to support. Another is that allocation of the costs will promote line division pressure for group overheads to be held in check. One argument for cost allocation that definitely must be resisted is that of obfuscation, where everyone knows that overheads are 'bad' and allocation sweeps them under the carpet.

To put cost allocation into perspective, consider two simple examples. A company occupies several floors of a building, yet it only makes one cheque each quarter for the rental payment. It is useful to allocate some of that rental cost to the various departments that use the building as they have control over the amount of floor space they use. Seeing the rental cost on their monthly cost report reminds them that there is a cost implication in their actions, even if any spare floor space cannot be sublet at short notice.

In the same company there is also a personnel department, with a manager responsible for its costs and performance. Allocation of the personnel department's costs to numerous user departments is highly likely to reduce control, as the costs become nobody's responsibility whereas before at least one person could monitor and control the costs. It is stretching the imagination to think that the line divisions are going to harass the personnel department about the relatively small costs that it would recharge to each of its clients.

In summary, transfer pricing and cost allocation are similar in substance. Since both are clerically demanding and can serve either to confuse or to improve the decision process, they should be employed only where there is a clear case that they will improve the control and understanding of costs. If in any doubt of the benefits, do not recharge or allocate and then at least the clerical effort has been saved.

Organization Restructures

> The financial controller wants to be involved in planning organizational changes. I can't see it is any of his business.

It is not too hard to devise complex organizational structures to meet the needs of customers, but it is another matter to be able to control those complex structures and, in particular, to reorient the reporting systems. Consider a business that up to now has been organized geographically, with a sales manager in each major town reporting through to a national manager. The reporting systems have been set up to reflect these managerial responsibilities and are working well.

Then market pressures force the company to reorganize itself with a split between retail customers and large commercial customers. Although all the business is delivered through the same distribution network, there are now two managers at most large sites, both reporting to different national managers: the national retail manager and the national corporate manager. In some small towns, the one local manager reports to both national managers. This change has to be reflected in a completely revised reporting system which will require many months of computer system reprogramming in order to segregate sales and stock into the new divisions of responsibility.

The issue is then whether to delay the reorganization until the reporting systems can cope with it. By delaying the reorganization, the business is continuing to operate in a way that is considered out of date. The delays may be lengthy as major systems redevelopment can take months or years, especially if altering old and fragile systems. This redevelopment work will also raise the issue of whether it is better to install a brand new system than to patch up old systems, and research on this topic will further delay the changes.

Should the reorganization proceed immediately, one of two things will happen. Either there will be much manual work to overcome the drawbacks of the computer systems and to provide some stopgap management reporting, or the business will continue without a proper management control system and consequently will have no way of knowing the impact of the new organization structure. The alternatives of delays, manual systems and no reporting system are all highly undesirable. Therefore the accounting staff must ensure they have a say in organizational issues to be able to warn senior management if the new organization structure cannot be supported by adequate reporting systems.

10

Budgets, Plans and Forecasts

Budgeting is the technique of converting operational targets into financial targets. It can be a powerful tool for control both initially, in going through the thought processes to prepare and justify the budget, and later, as a benchmark to evaluate actual performance. Budgeting can also be a thorough waste of time.

Before making any radical decisions to abandon or amplify the budgeting system, it is worth contemplating whether the process is in fact more important than the end result. The process involves considering the future, looking at alternatives and quantifying the preferred options: as such it is worthwhile effort, even if subsequent events differ radically from the budget. The alternative view is that these are management functions that should be happening continuously and that a budgeting process is an artificial contrivance to force these functions into one small part of the year.

The considerable effort spent on the budgeting process has to be outweighed by the intangible benefits that will come from improved control. The traditional budgeting systems have to be constantly questioned and updated. Budgets should not be merely accepted as a necessary evil in corporate life, one which many businesses could adequately survive without by routinely comparing actual results to those of the previous year or key indicators of trends in performance. The budgeting function also needs to be actively managed by senior executives. They have to keep their ear to the ground and try and discern whether the budgeting function has evolved into a process of apparent effectiveness rather than genuine aid to managing the business. It is not good enough to go through the motions of budgeting merely because it is a conventional part of business management.

Targets, Forecasts, Budgets and Plans

We tend to get tangled up between what we really expect to happen and what we hope will happen. This is reflected in a confusion in the budgets that we use.

The terms 'targets', 'forecasts', 'budgets' and 'plans' are often used interchangeably. Clarification is necessary within a company as confusion on the purpose of the process will be reflected in wasted effort in preparing the budget and understanding the results. An *operational plan* is a set of physical operations designed to bring about certain objectives: as such it need not be set in financial terms. For example, the operational plan might be to open ten new branches and hire another 200 staff. A *forecast* is the best estimate of the future based on a set of assumptions reflecting operational plans and external influences. As an example, the forecast might be for a growth in sales of 16%, given the opening of ten new branches and an expected general growth in demand of 7%.

A *target* is a statistical or financial objective that people should aim for and is imposed from within the company. It is usually based on a forecast, although the target can be set higher than the forecast. The target for the sales staff might be set at a 20% volume increase even though the forecast is for only a 16% overall increase. The *budget* is the financial representation of targets: it is the expenditure or contribution that managers are constrained by or are expected to achieve. In this example, the budget might be for sales of $200 million, reflecting the 20% sales growth target.

Medium-term Plans

The twelve-month financial planning horizon is too short in our line of business where projects take three years to come on stream.

Planning horizons typically extend the higher one moves up the organization structure. The chief executive is looking three to five years ahead, a line division manager one to two years ahead, a unit manager up to one year ahead and a production supervisor at the near future. So the twelve-month budgeting cycle is a compromise that suits only a few of the participants.

Many businesses conduct a 'medium-term plan' with a horizon

of three to five years. It has to be strategic to be of any use: that is, it must be a consideration of major operational decisions, such as to expand certain activities, to curtail others or to engage in organizational restructuring. Although strategic planning is a constant process, at some stage it is worthwhile documenting the current views in order to crystallize diverse opinions and communicate them to others. Input to the long-term plan has to be restricted to those who have a clear view of the future and can quantify that view, and this would probably be a small number of senior executives.

There is no one correct way of formulating a medium-term plan. It is up to the individual business to develop a process that suits its own circumstances. Whatever the process, the place to start is deciding what will be the output of the planning process, and from this one can work back to decide on the inputs. Typically the outputs of a medium-term plan should be a coherent set of business strategies, guidelines on how to implement those strategies and estimates on the impact of those strategies over the next, say, three to five years. An example of an output from a medium-term plan would be:

Vacuum Pumps Division Medium-term Plan
We will double our market share in the light industrial segment within four years. This will be achieved by using existing spare capacity. We will gradually move out of the education market segment. Market share will be obtained by aggressive pricing and marketing techniques and sales margins will have to be reduced to 25%. However, increased volumes will lead to 28% return on capital employed at the end of four years.

In this example the chief executive is able to say what he wants and, to some extent, how it should be achieved. He is then turning over the challenge to his subordinates to make it happen. This now provides a convenient starting point to set the annual budget for sales, costs and capital expenditure. If this is what is wanted from a medium-term plan, it becomes possible to specify the type of information and decision process needed to achieve the strategy statement.

Pursuing the above example further, the efficient approach would be for the vacuum pumps manager to provide a set of options to the chief executive, including the manager's preferred option. This could take the form of a stand-up presentation plus a pre-circulated booklet of background information. After receiving various proposals and options from all the individual business units, it is up to the chief executive, perhaps supported by a strategic planning specialist, to decide on the best strategy. Perhaps all the options will need more capital than can be afforded or, when aggregated, the overall profit result is unsatisfactory. This is where the chief executive has to earn his money, by deciding on the best options or taking unilateral decisions that were never offered as options, such as selling a part of the business. It is also likely that, in a closely integrated business, there will be inconsistencies or opposing points of view, and these need to be untangled before the total strategy can be released.

Executive Comment

> Too often the executive comment that I receive is obviously written by the divisional accountant. This doesn't tell me whether the divisional manager knows what is going on.

The management reporting system, when combined with executive comment, is a powerful tool for communication, rigorous control of the business and approval of business decisions. The process is only as good as the senior management force it to be. If they accept superficial comments or fail to follow up on comment from previous reports, then the system will decline and lose its usefulness.

For the division manager to be able to explain results to a superior, the reports and variance analysis prepared by the accountant must be examined and more analysis or investigation called for where a particular problem exists. For example, it may be necessary to call for a comparison to last year or a detailed analysis of reject rates. The division manager then has to describe the problem in business terms – not accounting jargon – saying whether remedial action is required. If the manager knows what action is required, that action should be specified. Alternatively, the manager should say that the matter is being investigated and that a more detailed report will follow at a later stage. It then requires the manager's superior to ensure this matter is followed up in due course.

The management report in figure 10.1 gives two commentaries on the same data. The first commentary is positively misleading as it says, by omission, that all is well. It suggests that the manager

	Budget	Actual	Variance
Sales	600,000	800,000	200,000
Cost of sales	(220,000)	(430,000)	(210,000)
Gross profit	380,000	370,000	(10,000)
Gross margin	63%	46%	
Less			
Salaries and wages	120,000	130,000	(10,000)
Advertising	80,000	50,000	30,000
Freight	40,000	75,000	(35,000)
Accommodation	35,000	35,000	0
Agency fees	25,000	0	25,000
Expenses	300,000	290,000	10,000
Contribution	80,000	80,000	0

Figure 10.1   Pump & Hose Trading Co., Western Region: operating report for Mar. 19X9 ($)

Initial Comment: The contribution for the month is right on plan, largely due to the excellent sales effort in attracting a new major wholesale customer which generated $200,000 in extra sales. Expenses have been carefully controlled and are $10,000 below budget. The $80,000 contribution is a favourable result given the very competitive market at present.

Informed Comment: Although we achieved budget profit for the month, there are a few issues to be commented on. We have lost the agency for Excel Pumps and we are running down existing stocks. Loss of this agency is a severe blow and we are searching for an alternative. On a trial basis we have started supplying Large Contracting Inc. However, the margins are greatly reduced, and after increased freight costs we are servicing this customer at a loss. We are hoping to expand the margin once we have proved our reliability to them. In view of our problems, we have cut back on advertising expenditure, but we cannot continue this for long. Profit outlook for the near future is bleak and alternative agency and marketing opportunities are being actively sought.

either is concealing the problems or else does not know they exist. It could be that the corporate culture is one of only reporting good news and inhibits the discussion of problems. If so, this is a management problem, not an accounting problem.

The second commentary officially comunicates that problems exist. It also demonstrates that the line manager understands what is happening and presumably has control over the business. It acts as a medium for approval of the action to be taken to remedy the situation. The line manager after submitting the report would assume that the specified actions and intentions have been approved unless notified otherwise.

Budget Options

The annual budget does not display the various options available to us to achieve our goals. I don't necessarily want to review all those options myself, but I want to know that the line managers have considered various options.

Traditional budgeting techniques are frequently based on the assumption that whatever happened last year will continue next year, only it will cost 10% more. This is an entirely unhelpful approach as it entrenches old ways of doing things. Two techniques have been developed to provide a more disciplined approach to the setting of budgets, namely:

- priority plan budgeting system (PPBS): this requires budget proposals to comprise alternative levels of service, the alternatives then being ranked in terms of their priority before deciding on the budget;
- zero-based budgeting (ZBB): this requires each year's budget proposals to start from the ground up, in effect justifying the function's existence.

As PPBS is probably the technique most relevant to the business environment, an extended example is shown. In this example, the Field Maintenance Department (part of the Engineering Services Division) has a group of mobile service technicians doing work within the organization. They can repair the units on site or remove the unit and send it to the factory. Its budget proposal is set out in figure 10.2. No decision is made on the Field Maintenance budget proposal until the options for all the other functions are considered. The summarized options for the Engineering Division are shown in figure 10.3.

The summarized options show that the $1.125 million guideline for spending will mean cuts of $133,400 ($1,258,400 minus $1,125,000) from the preferred options. There are $287,800 of

	Option 1: Minimum acceptable	Option 2: Preferred choice	Option 3: High quality
Service Level	6 hour response to faults	2 hour response to faults	Immediate response
Required Capital			
Vehicles	80,000	120,000	100,000
Repair equipment	40,000	60,000	0
Spare units	0	0	350,000
	120,000	180,000	450,000
Revenue Costs			
Labour	225,000	325,000	250,000
Components	10,000	10,000	0
Outside repairs	5,000	5,000	75,000
Depreciation	24,000	36,000	70,000
	264,000	376,000	395,000
Funding @ 18%	21,600	32,400	81,000
Operating costs	285,600	408,400	476,000
Possible Saving	122,800	Higher Option	67,600

Figure 10.2 Engineering Services Division, Field Maintenance Dept: budget options for the year ended 31/12/X5

Note: The funding cost @ 18% is the firm's investment hurdle rate applied to the capital required.

Department	Preferred option	Possible savings	Higher options
Technical Advisory Service	110,000	110,000	0
Technical Drawing Service	80,000	10,000	50,000
Factory Maintenance	250,000	20,000	100,000
Field Maintenance	408,400	122,800	67,600
Equipment Installation	305,000	0	0
Administration	105,000	25,000	0
Preferred spending	1,258,400		
Possible savings		287,800	
Higher options			217,600
Imposed Spending Limit	1,125,000 (Growth of 15% on last year)		

Figure 10.3 Engineering Services Division: budget priority worksheet for the year ended 31/12/X5

feasible savings, with major savings available in the Field Maintenance Department ($122,800) and by the closure of the Technical Advisory Service ($110,000). So achieving the $133,400 cuts boils down to either restricting the Field Maintenance budget or else closing the Technical Advisory Service.

The benefit of this approach is that it makes unit managers look at their options and quantify them. It then allows a rational analysis of what should be cut or improved. While it involves quite a bit of effort and paperwork, this would be reflected in a systematic allocation of resources. Unfortunately it does not necessarily show what the final budget will be. In the example, the Technical Advisory Service will probably be disbanded. This will not happen at the flick of a switch as it will take several months to redeploy the staff, and this factor will have to be adjusted for in the final budget.

The difference with the zero-based budgeting approach is not one of forms design or mathematics; it merely requires that activities are re-justified each year. In practice the main benefit should be to force a manager to look at alternatives, such as merging with another activity to reduce costs and improve performance, or subcontracting work instead of doing it in-house. These are options that should constantly be under review and not raised just as part of the budgeting process. In government accounting systems ZBB may have its place, particularly if it identifies a redundant function, such as one established to ensure compliance with legislation long since repealed.

Programme Budgets

We have a reporting system centred around managerial responsibility, but we wish to plan and track individual projects that span the whole organization.

Because most accounting systems are organized to support responsibility accounting, it makes it difficult to track and control activities, or programmes, that span numerous responsibility centres. *Programme budgeting* is a concept that requires budget proposals to cut across departmental boundaries. Although it was originally developed for government programmes, it can still be of relevance to support functions of a large departmentalized business. For example, consider a large organization that has decided that one of its major strategies will be to improve customer service. The board has agreed that $20 million of additional expenditure should be budgeted for implementation of the strategy. It needs to know that the additional money is being spent on this strategy rather than salted away into various unrelated projects.

The control system is bound to be imprecise in that the strategy will permeate through many departments and activities, for example:

- upgrading the switchboards;
- providing customer help-desks;
- improving computer response times;
- providing additional training for front-office staff;
- providing out-of-hours service teams;
- increasing inventory levels.

To monitor the impact of the customer service programme, the budgeting mechanism can be amended to require all managers to include specific proposals to improve customer service. These proposals would be summarized using the PPBS technique and given priorities in terms of their effectiveness in meeting the strategy while remaining within the total $20 million allowance. Therefore the normal budgeting process proceeds as usual, with programme budgets tacked on as a supplementary feature.

The difficulty is then in measuring results. While statistical and customer survey indicators can be installed to measure the effectiveness of the programme, the costs are unlikely to be properly measurable as they will become mixed in with normal operational expenses and development programmes. Lack of strict measurement of actual costs is a drawback but does not invalidate the attempt to allocate resources rationally at the outset of the project.

Top Down or Bottom Up

> I want a planning process that is both efficient and yet involves participation from all levels of management. These requirements seem to be mutually exclusive.

The process of setting budgets reflects to a great extent the management style of the business. While some businesses are run in an autocratic style ('do this'), others are more democratic. Leaving aside the argument of which is the better way to manage a business, when it comes to setting budgets it is necessary to recognize that alternative methods are available and that there are strengths and weaknesses in each approach.

At the extreme ends of the budgeting spectrum are the *top-down approach* (autocratic style) and the *bottom-up approach* (democratic style). In practice most firms would try to use the best of both worlds and the following comments should identify what balance is appropriate to an individual business.

The top-down approach relies on there being a person at a senior level of the organization who can say 'Here is the required target, now draw up a budget that will meet or surpass that target.' This target then filters down through the organization to the lowest manager. This is efficient in that it reduces the debate involved in negotiating targets up and down through varying levels of management. It also reflects the reality that the chief executive would be reluctant to accept any budget combination that does not meet the group's performance requirement. It is also positive in that it signals that senior management know what they want.

However, the target may be out of touch with realities that are only known at lower levels of the organization. If the targets are too low, they could install a benchmark for low performance. The targets may also be blindly followed, with budgets 'engineered' to give the target result: this invalidates the budgeting process by turning it into a mathematical exercise rather than a management exercise.

The bottom-up approach involves starting the budgeting process at the lowest managerial level and gradually aggregating the budgets to show the total. The budget total is then compared to the target and, if there is a shortfall in required profit, either it is accepted or else the process repeated until the correct answer is offered. This approach provides a budget that reflects the expectations of junior managers who are near to the market and the shop floor. It also requires junior managers to assess the future carefully and to create a sound plan, resulting in a higher commitment to achieving the budget. However, junior managers may not know, understand or sympathize with certain key strategies, and so these strategies could be omitted from the plan.

The bottom-up budget can incorporate a bias, with the type of bias reflecting the culture of the organization. Some organizations are naturally conservative (engineering managers?) and some naturally optimistic (sales managers?). This bias can then be magnified as budgets progress upwards through the management hierarchy, with each engineering manager chopping a bit off the budget and each sales manager adding on a bit more. This attempt at democratic management of the company is bound to be inefficient when at some stage the aggregate view of the line managers is found to be out of line with the targets that the chief executive wants to achieve. The chief executive is certain to ask the line divisions to have another go at their budgets and see if they can squeeze a bit more profit or delay some expenditure.

In practice, most organizations would try to combine the best of both alternatives by taking the top-down approach as far as, say, divisional level, and within a division attempting to gain a bottom-up budget through an iterative process. If the first attempt at the bottom-up budget does not meet the top-down target, there will have to be further research and negotiations to secure commitment to a higher target. Should the division agree that it can meet or exceed the target, no problems exist. If the division is convinced it cannot reach the target, there will have to be negotiation with the next level of management on how to resolve the shortfall: presumably any unresolved shortfall would then be reflected in the total group's annual plan.

It is essential to decide on the budgeting approach to be used before starting the process. When negotiation is to be a legitimate part of the agreement of budgets, sufficient timing must be allowed for this to occur. There also has to be a definite time at which the negotiation stops and the budget is finally settled.

Planning Gaps

> Every year we end up with a budget gap. Last year we bickered for two months over who would take up the shortfall. This year, if the budget isn't settled by the end of November, then ...

Whether top down or bottom up, there may be gaps in the budget, meaning that the sum of the parts adds up to more or less than the whole. There are two alternative views on how this should be managed. One is that the budget reflects a cohesive plan and all parts of the organization should be clear on their exact requirements: that is, the budget must add up. The other view is that the budget reflects differing views, there is insufficient time to reconcile all those views (i.e. to make the budgets add up) and in fact there is no need to do so even if there is sufficient time.

The more important aspects are whether the gap is favourable or unfavourable and how the gap is explained and managed. If the gap is favourable – that is, the lower levels of the organization are predicting better performance than top-level requirements – then there is no problem. The senior executives need to know that the gap exists, but then would presumably be happy for the line divisions to aim to outperform the group plan.

If the gap is unfavourable, then it is an issue that should be addressed before final agreement on the budget. It would be handled on a negotiated basis, with the chief executive trying to persuade the line divisions that higher targets are achievable. In this process, the reasons for the unfavourable gap would be highlighted. If the differences remain unresolved, the chief executive has a management problem in that he or she will be making a commitment to the board that is not supported by an equivalent commitment from the line divisions.

Division	Divisional budget	Planning gap	Official target	Actual results
Construction	900	50	950	860
Agency operations	320	0	320	330
Offshore contracts	1,020	(100)	920	1,050
	2,240	(50)	2,190	2,240

Figure 10.4   Maritime Supplies Company: contribution summary for February year to date ($000)

Department	Approved budget	Actual results	Variance
Consulting services	200	210	10
Equipment sales	1,000	1,100	100
Maintenance contracts	600	400	(200)
Planning gap	200		(200)
	2,000	1,710	(290)

Figure 10.5   Diesel Technics Inc.: contribution summary for November year to date ($000)

Two alternatives for reporting the budget gap are shown in figures 10.4 and 10.5. The first alternative is where individual divisions differ from a centrally prepared guideline. The second alternative is where there is only a total gap resulting from a bottom-up budget, although this begs the question as to which divisions differ from the centrally prepared budget. Planning gaps are messy and can call into question the integrity of the whole exercise: they should be avoided if possible.

Flexible Budgets

> The manufacturing divisions have developed superior techniques in flexible budgeting and I would like to see these applied to all other divisions.

The term *flexible budgeting* is a misnomer as it has connotations of a budget that somehow changes during the financial year. In fact what is really meant is that, when the budget is prepared, there is some measure of output that can be used for deciding on the resource to be consumed. *Output budgeting* is a more meaningful title and is used hereafter in lieu of flexible budgeting.

Manufacturing industries have been leaders in developing output budgeting because they have a tangible measure of output and financial accounting conventions have forced them to value this output in money terms, often using 'standard costs'. Lessons can be learnt from the manufacturing industries by the labour-intensive service industries which frequently also have a tangible measure of output.

Too often in service industries or service departments, the budget is developed based on inputs: for example, 'I need fourteen people, at $50,000 per annum each, plus $150,000 in overhead expenses.' This begs the questions, why fourteen? what is your workload? how many would you need if your workload increased by 50%? Further questions will arise later in the year when there are actually twenty-one people in the department instead of the fourteen predicated in the budget.

A far more disciplined budget and control mechanism would be developed if that departmental manager was able to justify inputs in correlation to required outputs. The manager could then say, 'I prepared my budget on the assumption from the sales department of us servicing 380 requisitions per day. We are now servicing 570 per day and that is why I need 50% more staff and that is why I will exceed my budget by 38%.'

This approach is an important element in *responsibility reporting* systems, whereby managers are held accountable only for matters which they can control. Clearly in the above example, the increased volume of requisitions, resulting from a successful sales drive, was not a matter that was controllable by the person who had to respond to the increased workload. Although the budget was overspent, the manager was probably doing a grand job in supporting a profitable increase in the sales volume.

It should be noted that the manager's original budget has not changed: that is, it is not a flexible budget. But the manager has a valid explanation of why the budget is being exceeded. If the manager's budget, and presumably that of many other service departments, was indeed flexible, then it would be a bureaucratic nightmare trying to control the constantly shifting benchmark.

Simple Claims: These take an average time of 2.5 hours of clerical labour:
   10,000 of these claims are predicted for next year.
Complex Claims: These take an average time of 8.0 hours of clerical labour:
   2,500 of these claims are predicted for next year.

	$
Labour Cost Estimation	
Salary cost p.a.	25,000
On-costs, such as payroll taxes and pension costs	
@ 15% salary	3,750
Supervision, rent, etc.	10,000
Annual cost of labour	38,750 per
	person
Hours available	
52 weeks @ 40 hours per week	2,080
Less: Holidays, sick leave, etc.	(280)
Less: Training and non-working time	(200)
Annual working time	1,600 hours
Cost Per Working Hour	
$38,750/1,600 hours	= 24.22 per
	hour

Budgeted Total Costs	$
10,000 simple claims @ 2.5 hours @ 24.22	605,500
2,500 complex claims @ 8.0 hours @ 24.22	484,400
Total Annual Budget	1,089,900

Figure 10.6   Quickpay Insurance Company, Claims Dept: budget worksheet

	Budget #	Actual #	Variance #
Simple claims	10,000	9,000	1,000
Complex claims	2,500	5,000	(2,500)
	$	$	$
Salaries	807,450	1,030,000	
Salary on-costs	114,300	147,000	
Stationery and postage	35,000	39,200	
Rent	105,000	204,300	
Sundry expenses	28,150	30,000	
Total Cost	1,089,900	1,450,500	(360,600)

Figure 10.7   Quickpay Insurance Company, Claims Dept: budget report for the year ended 31/12/X7

Manager's Comment: The over-budget position is entirely due to increased volumes of claims following the March hailstorms and flooding. If the work had been done at budgeted rates, it would have cost $1.513 million. Therefore this department has reduced its unit costs by 4% compared to the budget. The efficiencies were achieved by overtime work, temporary staff and temporary additional office space.

In figures 10.6 and 10.7, there is an example of output budgeting in use in the claims department of an insurance company. Figure 10.6 shows how the budget was derived and figure 10.7 shows how the department manager was able to demonstrate that, despite spending $360,600 more than the budget, the department's performance was cost-effective.

The output budgeting technique is worthwhile but relies on there being a tangible measure of output. In many service areas such measures do not exist, in which case PPBS provides a framework for deciding on the budget, although PPBS offers no means of explaining subsequent performance.

Changed Budget Assumptions

Copper prices have risen by 15% and the Wire Division is insisting that its budget has to be recast to reflect the new realities. Sounds plausible but I feel they should be still held to their original target.

In a budget influenced by one major financial assumption, for example a commodity price, changes in the assumption are not really a budgeting problem. Rather, it is a matter of to what extent the company wants to run with an unhedged risk, as it is possible to take forward positions on most major factors, such as commodities, interest rates and exchange rates. Therefore any variance between budget and actual results continues to be a fair comparison of performance.

There still remains the possibility that the budget contains a major flaw, or that circumstances have so radically changed that the budget is no longer relevant. Examples of this are where there is a major industrial dispute that closes the factory for two months, *force majeure* in an offshore subsidiary, loss of a major contract or unexpected government regulations. One option is to let the budget stand and spend the remainder of the year repeatedly explaining variances because of fundamental changes in the basis of the plan. Alternatively, the business could go through the trauma of doing the plan again and setting targets again in mid-stream. This in turn creates the problem of how to handle performance variances already reported for the first part of the year. It would be erroneous to let them stand, as they are based on a discredited budget, but it would also be pointless to redo the analysis using a budget prepared with the benefit of hindsight. The practical solution is to let the budget stand, warts and all, and to focus attention on forecasts of future performance and remedial action based on up-to-date assumptions.

If the budget becomes redundant in its components but is still valid in total because of organizational restructures, then the budget can be reallocated according to the new structure. Any spare budget or reorganization costs can be held centrally to give a true operating performance measure for the individual line divisions.

Commitment to Budgets

> The accountants seem to do all the budgeting work, and whenever there is a major variance the line managers can too easily blame the accountant. I want a much higher degree of involvement by the line managers: it is their budget, not the accountants'.

Budget setting is primarily an accountants' domain because they have been trained in the necessary skills and have a genuine interest in the topic. By contrast, many line managers see the budget as a necessary evil and wherever possible are willing to delegate the task to the nearest accountant. The danger is that the budgeting process becomes an accounting orgy and the underlying operational plans take second place. So there has to be a happy medium between accountants doing the specialist technical tasks and line managers specifying the assumptions and targets to be used. Reaching this happy medium is not a precise exercise, but there are ways of ensuring a high level of commitment from line management.

One method is to make the task dynamic and interesting for the line managers and so entice them to become more involved in preparing the budget. This can be achieved by creating personal computer budgeting models that allow the line managers to change various assumptions and promptly see the effect. Inexpensive spreadsheet software allows a complex model to be created while appearing to be fairly simple for a non-accounting user. If the line managers have had a direct hand in the budget production then it is likely they will have a much higher level of commitment to the budgetary control process.

Another method of gaining involvement and commitment is to require line managers to perform unaided presentations of their budget to senior managers. Not only will line managers take a big interest in what they have to present but, having presented it, they will also feel a greater degree of responsibility for achieving the result.

Budget Timing

The annual budget and medium-term plan occur right in the middle of our busy season, and I think we should look at ways of rearranging things so that we can give it the priority it deserves.

Budgeting on an annual basis has evolved as the main focus because it accords with the financial year used for legalistic purposes. It also incorporates the four seasons and thus caters for seasonal business, such as the sale of ice-cream or skis. Although there is little realistic alternative to a twelve-month budgeting cycle, there is no need for the annual plan to coincide with the statutory accounting year, and in fact there may be good reasons to disconnect the two time spans.

Most large businesses have to prepare quarterly accounts such that there are effectively four unique accounting periods in the year. The budget can be prepared on a similar basis but out of phase by three months or six months. Figure 10.8 shows a budgeting cycle that is six months out-of-phase with the statutory financial year.

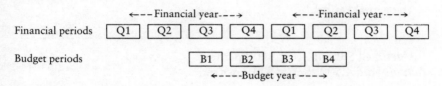

A quarterly budget is prepared which spans two financial years.

Figure 10.8 Phasing of budgets and financial periods

Variance Analysis

I find that many of the explanations on the operating reports are at odds with the numbers on the reports. Is there some way of tying together the words and the numbers?

Management reports are of little use unless they contain objective measures of comparative performance and explanations of changes. Comparisons can be made between:

- different accounting periods (actual this year versus actual last year);
- budget and actual results;
- latest estimate and the budget;
- one operating unit and another.

Objective analysis is greatly assisted if there are some fundamental measures of activity, such as the number of units made or sold, the number of tons of steel used, the amount of fuel used or the volume of rejects, for which the units price or cost can be derived. Armed with this detail, the differences between the two sets of results can be readily analysed. The analysis is termed *variance analysis* and has traditionally been taught by rote learning of complex formulae. In fact the calculations are fairly simple and can be derived from first principles providing there is a clear understanding of the objective of the exercise. The examples in figures 10.9, 10.10, 10.11 and 10.12 are included to demonstrate the principles.

Example 1: Volume and Price Variance   In figure 10.9, the variance of $5,000 is broken down into two components, both of which are quite large but which offset each other. This segregation into volume and price helps in explaining the difference between the budget and the actual results.

Budget: Sell 5,000 tons at $100 per ton
Actual: Sold 4,500 tons at $110 per ton

Management Report

	Budget	Actual	Variance
Sales	$500,000	$495,000	($5,000)

Variance Explanation
500 tons less than plan have been sold.
This loss is 500 × $100

Volume Variance	(50,000)

However, $10 per ton extra was gained on
the actual sales, 4,500 × $10

Price Variance	45,000
Total Variance	($5,000)

Figure 10.9   Example 1: Volume variance and price variance

Note: This analysis segregates the total variance into its two components.

Example 2: Yield Variance   The example in figure 10.10 shows the yield variance, which quantifies the benefit of a change in production techniques from one year to another. In this example, the level of inputs was increased (e.g. more power) and this was more than offset by a lower loss rate. The yield gain was $0.63 per kg when compared to the previous year.

Example 3: Efficiency Variance   The example in figure 10.11 is an exercise where the identical product of two factories is being compared to identify the more efficient plant. The word 'efficiency' is often restricted to an assessment of the usage of labour, but in this example it refers to all types of cost. It does not matter what terminology is used so long as it is used consistently within the one company.

	Last year			This year		
	Kg	$/kg	Cost ($)	Kg	$/kg	Cost ($)
Plastics	2,000	10	20,000	5,000	10	50,000
Additives	10	95	950	25	95	2,375
Power			4,000			15,000
Loss	−250			−50		
Output	1,760		$24,950	4,975		$67,375

Per-unit cost	$14.18 per kg	$13.55 per kg

Per-unit variance $14.18−$13.55 = $0.63 per kg
Total saving (*Yield Variance*)=$0.63×4,975 kg = $3,134

Figure 10.10   Example 2: Yield variance

Note: Improvements in the plastics process are compared to performance in the last year.
The last year's results have been restated at this year's prices to remove any price
change effects. Despite using proportionately more power this year, the yield
improvement is an effective saving of $3,134.

	North Factory		South Factory	
	Inputs	$	Inputs	$
Skilled labour (hrs)	150	4,500	200	6,000
Unskilled labour (hrs)	60	1,320	20	440
Machine usage (hrs)	80	8,000	100	10,000
Materials (kg)	2,000	20,000	1,900	19,000
Packing materials		500		600
		34,320		36,040
Per-unit cost		34.32		36.04

Figure 10.11   Example 3: Efficiency variance

Note: The identical products of two factories are compared to identify the more efficient
plant, using a batch of 1,000 units. The price of inputs has been adjusted to be the
same in both cases. The factories use different mixes of skilled and unskilled labour.
South uses more machine time and has less materials wastage. The overall result is
that North is more efficient by $1.72 (5%) per unit.

Example 4: Price (or Rate) Variance   The example shown in figure 10.12 compares budgeted prices with actual prices to reveal the price or rate variances.

	Budgeted rates	*Actual*	*Price or rate variance*
Labour	$28 per hour	100,000 hours @ $28.50	($50,000) u
			(i.e. 100,000 hours @ $0.50)
Fuel oil	$260 per ton	4,000 tons @ $230	$120,000 f
			(i.e. 4,000 tons @ $30)
Steel	$380 per ton	7,000 tons @ $400	($140,000) u
			(i.e. 7,000 tons @ $20)

Figure 10.12   Example 4: Price variance

Note: The effect of changing prices is calculated for major inputs.
   u = unfavourable variance; f = favourable variance.

These examples of variance analysis show that, using simple mathematics, it is possible to generate additional understanding of how things have changed between one set of results and another. This is the type of analysis that accountants should provide to line managers, who then take the responsibility to explain the underlying business reasons for the change.

11

Profit Motivation

Investment in a business is done so as to receive a return. Two major decision processes are required: firstly, how to make a sound investment and secondly, how to manage the investment to receive a payback. This chapter looks at how a chief executive can control and motivate the business so that the payback is optimized, thereby ensuring both personal and business success.

Profit Recognition

> I want everybody in the company to understand the importance of profit. It's their future but they seem to want to give it away to the customer.

Profit, in the broadest sense of the word, represents the shareholders' reward for risking their money in the company. The maintainable profits of a company are vital to its ability to fund expansion through retained earnings or by attracting additional investment. Profit attempts to reflect the value added by the company's activities, being the difference between the value of inputs of raw materials and labour and the value of outputs passed to the customer. High profits denote the ability of the company to add more value than its competitors and are something to be proud of.

There is no correct level of profitability. However, competitive pressures tend to limit profits within an industry segment and low profitability eventually drives firms out of business by bankruptcy or forced mergers. The aim of every firm should be to outperform its competitors by ensuring the long-term maintenance of profits, sometimes at the expense of short-term profits.

Contribution

> I think the word 'contribution' is entirely appropriate to the way we manage our business. People contribute to the success of their department; departments contribute to the success of their division; divisions contribute to the success of the company.

Using profit motivation within the company is highly desirable as it gives a simple primary focus for employees. However, profit can be difficult to measure at lower levels of the organization and can be too simplistic in certain cases. Profit is a measure that has to be used with caution. *Contribution* is a term used interchangeably with profit. It can be thought of as a lower level of profit, in that various units each make a contribution and the sum of these contributions is the total profit. Contribution should also comprise only those items of income and expenditure directly attributable to an individual management area. The concept of contribution is demonstrated in the simplified profit and loss account shown in figure 11.1, where each division makes a contribution to the corporate overheads and net profit.

Northern Division contribution	1,000
Southern Division contribution	2,000
Western Division contribution	(500)
Divisional contributions	2,500
Less: Corporate overheads	(500)
Net profit	2,000

Figure 11.1   Regional Distributing Corporation: operating summary for October ($000)

Contribution can give a rose-tinted view of life in businesses with a large volume of central costs. In figure 11.1, for example, the manager of Southern Division could claim to be responsible for 100% of the company's profit. To counter this there is a natural temptation to allocate the central costs to the line divisions, when the more correct action is to investigate why there is such a high level of spending by head office, or whether many head

	Income	Costs	Contribution
Sales Dept	6,000	(3,100)	2,900
Distribution Dept	0	(600)	(600)
Purchasing Dept	0	(200)	(200)
Administration	0	(100)	(100)
Total	6,000	(4,000)	2,000

Figure 11.2   Southern Division: operating summary for October ($000)

office functions should be streamlined or devolved to the line divisions.

The previous example gave a reasonable indication of where value (i.e. profit) is being added in the business process, but attempts to follow the trail further down the organization can be difficult. The operating statement for Southern Division in figure 11.2 shows the problem. This report superficially indicates that all the value is being added by the sales department, when really the value is being added by an excellent purchasing function that locates suppliers at costs well below the industry average. This leads to the issue of transfer pricing, whereby the purchasing department might charge the sales department with the market price for the raw materials. Compared to base cost, this would show the true contribution from the purchasing department. The vexed question of transfer pricing is discussed in more detail in chapter 9.

Peer Pressure

I realize profit or contribution measurement of the line divisions is inexact, but think where we would be without it: cost control would disappear and margins would fall.

Despite the inexactness of contribution measurement, there are behavioural forces within a company that can be harnessed to optimize overall profit. These forces are inter-departmental competition and peer pressure. To use these forces there has to be a contribution measurement system in place, albeit imprecise, which will make them surface and result in the company moving in the right direction.

Consider the simplified example of a company comprising:

- line divisions that sell the product to the customer using a national price list, with some local discretion for discounting;
- a central Marketing Group that sets the national price list, performs market research, designs new products and manages the advertising campaign.

Although the line divisions can readily be considered as profit centres, their results are influenced by the ability of the Marketing Group to read the market and set prices accordingly. The influence of the Marketing Group is so fundamental as to overshadow any fiddling with the accounting system through transfer pricing subtleties. Therefore the financial reporting system should be left alone and reliance has to be placed on the human interaction between the line managers and the Marketing Group.

These interactions will take the form of the line divisions exerting pressure on the Marketing Group to provide a high level of support. To provide this support, the Marketing Group will have to listen to what the line divisions have to say about what the customers want and the price they are willing to pay. Unless the line divisions are being tightly measured on their profit performance, they may not have the motivation to pressure other parts of the company to perform. Despite the management reporting system being simplistic, its existence serves to make the business go in the correct direction.

Peer pressure can have a major influence where there are a number of similar-sized divisions in the same line of business. Not only are managers competing against the external market, but they are also competing with each other in an objective and positive sense. This factor can be used to advantage, especially when setting performance targets or when seeking solutions to technical problems.

Particularly in firms with complex inter-divisional dependencies that cannot be fully reflected in the management reporting systems, the chief executive has a vital role in making the system work: initially by establishing a management style that allows healthy dispute and its resolution, then by umpiring the process and discerning where the real problem exists, and lastly by ensuring that any profit-based bonus system reflects, at least partly, the health of the whole group and not just sectional interests.

Limitations on Profit Measurement

> All of my people know what is expected of them, and if I can keep them all going at 100% then I will be beating the competitors and doing the right thing for the stockholders. I don't need monthly profit reports to tell me who is, and is not, working hard.

Opponents of profit centre accounting argue that experienced managers should know all the elements that make a business profitable, and if they do each of these to the best of their ability then good profits will follow. Whilst there is some merit in this approach in a small business, a profit centre reporting system will serve as a periodic reminder of the relative importance of various elements, so countering a manager's personal bias. For example, the manager might consider that tight control of packaging costs is vital, whereas in the total picture it could be far less important than controlling inventory levels. Periodic review and explanation of a contribution statement helps to highlight the relative importance of the steps in the business process.

The 'I'm doing my best' argument also contains a fallacy in that it ignores the outside world. Doing one's best may not be good enough when competitors are doing even better or when customers need to be persuaded to pay a price sufficient to ensure a reasonable profit. Profit centre accounting, possibly accompanied by a market-based transfer pricing system, can expose many parts of the firm to the reality of competitors and to the customers' perception of price and performance.

Care is needed to avoid taking profit centre accounting beyond its limits. A classic example concerns maintenance activities where performance, for safety reasons, is far more important than profit considerations. Even without safety considerations it is too easy to make short-term profit improvements at the expense of premature equipment failure caused by reduced maintenance. In such cases control is needed, but it should be based on technical standards and statistical measures rather than on simplistic cost reductions.

Investing in Future Profits

> Since introducing profit targets and bonuses there have been some significant cuts in spending, but I worry whether we are jeopardizing the future.

In most businesses it is tempting to improve short-term profits at the cost of longer-term improvements. Typical examples are reductions in research and development spending, maintenance spending and staff development programmes. There may also be a tendency to reject small (and unprofitable) customers that may one day grow into big customers. This is exacerbated in reporting systems that can only measure current (short-term) profitability. The problem is how to counteract this tendency while still keeping a strong profit motivation.

Alternatives exist, one of which is in the organization design, whereby development and maintenance functions are kept away from line management's control so that they do not become the focus of short-term cost-cutting exercises. It is then vital that the development and maintenance functions have some performance measures to ensure they continue to be good value for money.

Another approach is to set managerial objectives that balance profit with objectives that take a long-term perspective. Such objectives may be difficult to monitor properly, especially in relation to equipment maintenance, but at least they remind line managers that there are factors other than short-term profit on which they will be measured.

A more indirect approach is that of forcing the line managers to think ahead to set up the infrastructure for the future. This can be accomplished by having the managers develop medium-term plans that involve planning their:

- staffing needs;
- equipment replacement programmes;
- customer-base profile;
- factory capacity requirements.

There is no need to translate these plans into financial terms; in fact doing so might denigrate the process into a mathematical exercise instead of an exercise in resources planning. The act of making these long-term plans serves as a strong reminder that there has to be a balance between short-term profits and long-term growth.

External and Internal Reporting

I have little sympathy with the external reporting rules. We have to comply with them because that is the law, but they are not the right way for us to internally measure our business.

Before getting too carried away with the joys of profit, it is worth cautioning the business manager (if he or she does not already suspect it) that profit as it is portrayed to the outside world is a piece of accurate nonsense. Statutory profit is in effect an explanation of the difference between the balance sheet of one year and that of the next. A balance sheet is a hotchpotch of accounting jargon at odds with business reality. For example, what does 'amortized goodwill' mean? What is the relevance of the 'net book value of fixed assets'? What are 'retained earnings'? Where are the trademarks and patents for which a competitor would gladly pay $10 million? These questions can be answered only by saying that traditional external accounting is a convention and that most business managers are happy with this convention in that it tells investors and competitors little of practical use.

For routine reporting purposes within a business, profit, or better still contribution, is a useful measure, especially if its limitations are well understood and the more esoteric accounting concepts are weeded out and ignored. However, contribution measurement has to be supplemented with tight control over capital expenditure, inventories and debtors; the only absolute truth in business is cash flow, and it is too easy to look only at profits and to miss the signals of a looming cash crisis.

Integrity of Management Reports

> When I read the monthly management reports, I have to be sure that what I am seeing is the real profit and not some funny money that will disappear once the annual audit is done.

The accounting records serve two purposes: the external (financial) accounts and the internal management accounts. The requirements for these two purposes differ slightly in that petty detail is often required for statutory or taxation purposes. In addition to this, certain management accounting information is processed, such as cost allocations or transfers of stock with profit margins included ('transfer pricing'); for statutory purposes the unrealized profit on stock transfers has to be eliminated. Some of the management reporting concepts used for profit measurement may differ from the statutory accounting rules, and, as mentioned previously, it is desirable to ignore some of the esoteric statutory accounting concepts when measuring the individual operating units.

Chief executives are greatly interested in the statutory profit (albeit flawed in concept and in delivery) as this is the amount for which they are ultimately answerable. They are also interested in the system that measures the operating units under their control. So they need to receive the 'management accounting results' and a schedule that adjusts these to the statutory accounting results. The differences between the financial accounts and the management accounts must be progressively monitored and explained so that the chief executive is not confronted with a surprise change in profits when the statutory accounts eventually appear at the end of the year.

12

Control Without Budgets

A stated major aim of most financial reporting systems is to provide motivation for managers to work towards targets that accord with business strategies. The premise is that a budget is drawn up that reflects strategic and tactical goals, and periodic comparison of actual against the budget provides a measure of performance. Thus, when managers see a variance on their reports, they know that they may have to change their operations in some way to get back to the budget. Therefore companies make a large commitment to the budgeting process as the one time of the year when they can impose a discipline on the planning framework: vague notions have to be crystallized and competing views can be reconciled. It provides an opportunity for numerous managers to be brought up to date on the thoughts of the chief executive concerning how the business is to progress over the next year. It sounds good, but the theory is often better than the practical application and alternatives do exist.

Before going further, it must be stressed that there is a difference between budgets and forecasts, although most companies see that a budget serves both purposes. Forecasts are essential as they try to tell a business where it is really going, and a business has to know where it is really going if for no other reason than to plan its cash flow. Budgets only tell the business about where it wishes it were going, and this can be achieved without the elaborate budgeting process that is ingrained into most institutions.

The Purpose of Budgets

We are trying to cut back on costs in our administration and the budgeting function has to be high on the list of potential savings. It ties up most of our managers for several weeks each year and involves an army of accountants.

The first proposition in favour of budgets was that it forces a discipline on the planning process as it sets aside a certain time each year when managers get in a huddle and actually manage. The existence of a budget process that fosters this concept is counterproductive as it implies that for the rest of the year it is not necessary to co-ordinate the planning process, or that managers can go back to immersion in their operational systems and cease to be real managers. Hopefully planning is a constant process regardless of whether it is actually translated into and documented in financial terms.

A budgeting process can be useful for communicating strategies to line managers, but it is surprising that a company has to use such a devious route. It is more straightforward just to tell the line managers what they are supposed to do, instead of demanding that they spend time creating a budget.

The motivational impact of budgeting depends greatly on the complexity of the business and the ability of the underlying reporting system to explain budget variances. The system will be much more relevant to managers if they can easily explain variances in terms of their own actions than if variances are caused by unavoidable factors or controlled by the actions of others. Since businesses are becoming more integrated and complex, the motivation of the individual manager will gradually have to change to the motivation of a group of managers with joint responsibilities. Budgets will become less relevant in this environment and other forms of motivation will have to be sought.

The underlying problem with budgets as a motivational tool is that they become a game containing ambit claims and soft targets. Annual budgets can also impose inflexibility especially if priorities change during the year. People see the approved budget as a licence to do what the budget predicates, and if there is an attempt to amend the budget during the year then this is seen as a sign of indecision or bad management. Few businesses have the luxury of being able rigidly to lock in their expenditure priorities for twelve months, yet many are reluctant to scrap or amend the budget part of the way through the year.

On this basis the need for the traditional extensive budgeting process is dubious, although there is a pressing need for reliable forecasts. Only the chief executive of a company can decide whether to manage the business using budgets, but not many financial controllers would offer it as a serious option. A business can survive quite adequately without a budget.

Continuous Forecasting

If I remove the budgeting process, I want to be sure that I still have a mechanism to control the business.

Whether a budget is used or not, the main purpose of a financial reporting system has to be to indicate whether performance is improving or getting worse. If it is improving, can it be sustained? If it is deteriorating, what can be done to turn it around? These questions can be answered by using an integrated forecasting system.

An integrated forecasting system highlights trends rather than focusing heavily on the current month or an aggregate year-to-date performance. Furthermore, it attempts to provoke constant consideration of the future, as this is the only way to impact the health of the business. The emphasis is not on accountability; rather, it is on providing a framework to managers which can be used to tell both them and their superiors how the business is progressing.

The sample management reports in figures 12.1 and 12.2 are a demonstration of the principles of trend analysis and forecasting using an engineering business as an example. It does not matter whether it is a stand alone business or a segment of some larger business; the principles remain the same. The main focus is on identifying historical trends and then requiring managers regularly to forecast future results.

Obviously many permutations on the theme are possible and care must be taken not to get carried away with the profusion of fancy technology that is available. In figure 12.1, the costs related to the machine workshop are segregated into the labour costs and expenses. The labour productivity index is calculated as the ratio of actual manhours worked to the theoretically measured hours (standard allowance). Likewise the materials productivity index is the ratio of actual materials usage to the allowance for the work done. In principle, this is the same as the traditional standard costing technique; however, here there is no attempt to make any bookkeeping entries for the standard allowances or to represent

	Last six months						This month	Next six months					
	Jan.	Feb.	Mar.	Apr.	May	Jun.	month	Aug.	Sep.	Oct.	Nov.	Dec.	Jan.
Labour Costs													
Production time	1.02	1.00	1.08	1.20	1.25	1.12	1.15	1.20	1.20	1.25	1.26	1.30	1.35
Maintenance time	0.23	0.24	0.23	0.23	0.24	0.26	0.27	0.26	0.26	0.26	0.26	0.26	0.26
Development time	0.28	0.23	0.30	0.15	0.16	0.20	0.15	0.16	0.25	0.25	0.35	0.22	0.13
Unproductive time	0.20	0.19	0.21	0.21	0.21	0.21	0.20	0.21	0.22	0.23	0.24	0.23	0.23
	1.73	1.66	1.82	1.79	1.86	1.79	1.77	1.83	1.93	1.99	2.11	2.01	1.97
	← Growth on previous 6 months 5.3% →							← Growth on previous 6 months 8.9% →					
Expenses													
Production overheads	1.09	1.05	1.15	1.12	1.17	1.12	1.12	1.15	1.22	1.25	1.33	1.27	1.24
Rejected work	0.00	0.00	0.26	0.45	0.00	0.00	0.15	0.00	0.00	0.00	0.00	0.00	0.00
Waste materials	0.05	0.05	0.05	0.06	0.06	0.06	0.06	0.06	0.06	0.06	0.06	0.07	0.07
Maintenance costs	0.53	0.55	0.53	0.53	0.55	0.60	0.62	0.60	0.60	0.60	0.60	0.60	0.60
	1.67	1.65	1.99	2.16	1.79	1.78	1.95	1.81	1.88	1.91	1.99	1.93	1.90
	← Growth on previous 6 months 7.3% →							← Growth on previous 6 months 7.4% →					
Productivity Indices													
Labour	98%	97%	95%	90%	80%	85%	88%	95%	95%	95%	95%	100%	100%
Materials	87%	80%	77%	85%	90%	95%	96%	98%	98%	100%	100%	100%	100%
Capacity Indices													
Capacity index	79%	76%	83%	81%	85%	81%	81%	83%	88%	90%	96%	91%	89%
Work backlog (wks)	2	1	0	0	0	2	2	1	0	0	0	0	0
Forward orders (wks)	13	12	10	5	8	12	13	0	0	0	0	0	0

Figure 12.1 Machine workshop: operations report ($m)

the variance in financial terms. The capacity index relates the actual workload to the theoretical maximum available. Again this is obliquely represented in standard costing variance reporting by the under- or over-absorption of fixed costs.

Forward orders, expressed in weeks of capacity, are shown to help build a correlation between capacity planning and productivity. In this type of business, long-term scheduling of production can give significant savings in having to retool machines. The work backlog is also shown as an indicator of the ability to meet production targets. The forecast is then sent up through the organization, where it is amalgamated with forecasts from other parts of the business to provide the whole picture, and this is shown in figure 12.2.

The ability to perform reasonable forecasts for each of the ensuing six months depends greatly on the support systems available to the manager. Naturally some businesses are more predictable than others, but in any settled and established business there has to be a way of making informed estimates. Some of the indicators will be available from within the company, such as existing sales contracts and details of marketing campaigns. Other indicators will be external, such as the government statistics of new building approvals or consumer spending patterns. Pulling all these indicators together to form the basis for a business forecast is initially a daunting task, but once the systems and data correlations have been established the routine processing is straightforward. Whatever the level of detail or certainty of the forecasting indicators, there has to be an interpretation of the impact on each part of the business, and co-ordination by one person is required so that all related parts of the business are working under the same assumptions. Just where this co-ordinator is located is unimportant, be it in the sales or production or accounting department, but the person must combine a detailed knowledge of the business environment with statistical and accounting skills.

Having built up these forecasting skills, one might think that there is now the basis for some accurate annual budgeting. This would be to fall back into the trap of focusing on annual predictions instead of the continuous forecasting that implies continuous management and control. Under the control system being advocated here, since the reporting and forecasting procedure is repeated every month, the detailed knowledge of the business and refinement of the systems build up very quickly. There is no arbitrary financial year end that the operational managers have to

	Last six months						This month	Next six months					
	Jan.	Feb.	Mar.	Apr.	May	Jun.	month	Aug.	Sep.	Oct.	Nov.	Dec.	Jan.
Sales income	8.95	8.69	9.77	10.03	9.01	8.89	9.39	9.67	10.00	10.29	10.72	10.74	10.71
Cost of production	(2.10)	(2.04)	(2.15)	(2.27)	(2.10)	(2.00)	(2.13)	(2.39)	(2.39)	(2.49)	(2.51)	(2.73)	(2.84)
Workshop overheads	(2.38)	(2.31)	(2.73)	(2.75)	(2.40)	(2.44)	(2.57)	(2.44)	(2.61)	(2.65)	(2.85)	(2.64)	(2.52)
Purchasing	(0.24)	0.24	(0.24)	(0.24)	(0.24)	(0.24)	(0.24)	(0.24)	(0.24)	(0.24)	(0.24)	(0.24)	(0.24)
Marketing and sales	(0.35)	0.35	(0.35)	(0.35)	(0.35)	(0.35)	(0.35)	(0.35)	(0.35)	(0.35)	(0.35)	(0.35)	(0.35)
Contribution	3.89	4.93	4.30	4.43	3.92	3.86	4.11	4.25	4.41	4.56	4.77	4.78	4.77
Contribution per machine hour ($)	78	99	86	89	78	77	82	85	88	91	95	96	95
Development Costs													
Workshop	(2.51)	(1.10)	(0.15)	(0.47)	(1.04)	(0.58)	(0.22)					(0.30)	
Marketing		(0.11)	(0.13)	(0.04)					(0.25)				
Support	(0.03)	(0.04)	(0.01)					(0.21)		(0.45)	(0.45)	(0.09)	(0.10)
	(2.54)	(1.25)	(0.29)	(0.51)	(1.04)	(0.58)	(0.22)	(0.21)	(0.25)	(0.45)	(0.45)	(0.39)	(0.10)
Development costs as a % of contribution				24.51% (January to June)						6.52% (July to January)			
Forward orders (wks)	13	12	10	5	8	12	13						
Forward orders ($m)	28.2	26.0	21.7	10.8	17.3	26.0	28.2						

Figure 12.2 Engineering financial summary report ($m)

worry about. The process just keeps cycling through, month after month.

How the engineers actually use the information presented to them will depend greatly on their own abilities and perception of the key controllable factors. The reports do not spell out good or bad, although it is fairly evident that the aim must be to optimize the key ratios. Hopefully these reports are the catalyst for the engineers to seek further information that helps them manage the business: for example, statistics on staff turnover or reject rates on certain types of job.

Cost of Policy Decisions

> One of the main purposes of the reporting system is to keep a tight lid on costs. It is our prime method of implementing cost reductions.

Many managers assume that a good cost reporting system ensures control of costs. An astute observer has likened this to watching the scoreboard instead of watching the ball. The popular view is that having tight and accurate reporting systems makes people accountable for costs and motivates them to reduce their costs. It is more likely that, after a while, managers become immune to any embarrassment about their costs. They set an expenditure budget and, so long as they keep within the budget, they consider they are controlling costs. Although the budget process can be used to investigate costs, in substance cost reduction is achieved by a detailed and objective view of how things are done, accompanied by a genuine desire to reduce costs.

Inevitably, the drive for cost reduction arises from competition. Reducing costs is painful, requiring hard decisions about eliminating practices that some of the existing management were responsible for implementing. Without strong competition the pain can always be deferred just a little bit longer.

So the first step is to look for the major factors that influence costs. To do this one has to go past such simplistic answers as 'Labour is our major cost – we have too many staff.' This begs the question, what do the staff do and why? If it is unnecessary then stop it, and if it is necessary then work out a way to do it better. Accountants are not trained to do this investigation but they can support the process.

A certain level of cost is entrenched in a business at the design stage and further costs arise according to how the technology is used. So cost reduction has to operate at the design stage and during live operations. For example, it may be corporate policy for a certain type of uniform to be worn by the staff, and once that policy is set a certain level of costs is inevitable. Cost reduction has to occur when setting the policy by deciding on the purpose of the uniform and the quality needed to achieve that purpose. Although this involves subjective judgements on style and image and staff acceptance, the policy-maker should be aware of the cost impact of the decision. The policy-setting process must force consideration of the cost aspect and the options for achieving the same effect by other means. As a part of the process of making policy decisions, a cost impact statement should be produced and this can be used later to evaluate whether the actual costs are being constrained within the original view of costs versus benefits.

Product line complexity is also a major factor that influences costs. To cope with numerous variations on a basic product, there may have to be costly down time when retooling machines. There are also the additional costs imposed by training staff to cope with the exceptions to the rule, stocking slow-moving raw materials and spending management time juggling a more complex production schedule. Providing the customer is willing to pay for the full incremental cost of these complexities, there is no problem. However, under detailed examination, the full incremental cost can turn out to be much more than it superficially appears: only a thorough examination of live settled operations can really disclose the full incremental cost.

A more difficult example concerns the setting of maintenance policies. When the maintenance engineer decides that all the earth-moving machinery will be regularly painted with an expensive rust-preventing non-chip paint, a decision has been made that will affect future costs and also future benefits. Presumably the plant will need less frequent repainting and will have a higher resale value, but this will be countered by extra painting costs. As with the staff uniforms, there will be a high degree of subjectivity in the decision and in many companies there would be no attempt to articulate the net benefit of this maintenance policy. While it is impractical to expect all maintenance policies to be properly documented in terms of their costs and benefits, serious cost reduction can occur only by considering cost effectiveness at a micro level of detail. Sometimes it will be more cost effective to let the machinery rust than meticulously to repaint it each year; routine expenditure reports will never reveal which is the correct policy. So rather than rely on a bureaucratic cost control process which can easily be manipulated, the real answer rests with the management style of the business, in which hard-nosed cost decisions become embedded in every facet of the operations.

While there are serious limitations when looking at maintenance costs, the routine reporting system can provide broad measurement of the effect of cost reduction initiatives. This is not achieved by tracking total costs because business growth is likely to keep total costs increasing despite individual efficiency successes. Therefore the reporting system has to find some hard indicators of efficiency and concentrate on these even if it cuts across the traditional cost centre and standard costing reporting techniques. It is most likely that non-financial indicators are appropriate, providing these have a link to the movement in costs. The following list of examples demonstrates data that are normally readily available within a company and can be used to monitor cost effectiveness.

Purchasing, Stock Control and Distribution

Clerical Cost Per Purchase Order Processed   This indicates the average cost of making an order. It can be used to monitor the cost impact of purchasing system improvements and to set purchasing policies.

Warehouse Cost Per Annum Per Stockline   This indicates the cost of maintaining a stockline. It can be used for decisions on stockholding policies and pricing, or to monitor the cost impact of materials handling systems improvements.

Warehouse Cost Per Requisition Processed   This indicates the cost of picking and packing a requisition. It helps to highlight the cost of processing small orders.

Freight Cost Per Tonne-mile   This indicates the cost of distribution. It can be used for pricing decisions and in comparison with external contractors.

Stock Turnover   This indicates the length of time that stock stays in the warehouse. It provides an indicator of whether purchase quantities are excessive in relation to demand, but it has to be judged against the discounts available from bulk purchases.

Stock-outs Per Requisition   This indicates the number of times that there is no stock on hand. It reflects the ability of the purchasing department to predict demand and manage deliveries. It has to be balanced against the need not to carry too much stock, which would incur financing costs and an increased chance of spoilage.

Response Time Per Requisition   This indicates the elapsed time between receiving a requisition and issuing the stock. It reflects the efficiency of processing orders, although optimum cost efficiency may mean queuing requisitions and spreading the workload.

Maintenance and Engineering

Equipment Unscheduled Down Time   This indicates the extent to which machinery is unavailable other than during planned maintenance. It reflects the maintenance manager's ability to minimize breakdowns, although misuse by the operator can be a major factor.

Equipment Operating Cost Per Hour   This indicates the cost of using the machine for one hour and is important for product costing and evaluating the impact of new machines or changed methods.

Ratio of Planned to Unplanned Maintenance   Expressed in terms of down time, this indicates how much of the maintenance work results in lost production. In some areas no breakdowns are permissible for safety reasons, but generally a small amount of breakdown repairs is more cost effective than routine replacement of still serviceable parts: therefore a reasonable level of down time may be inevitable.

Personnel Administration

Staff Turnover   This indicates what proportion of the staff are leaving each year. This is a key indicator in that unwanted staff turnover is expensive in terms of replacement recruiting and training. It could also reflect poor hiring tactics, wage problems or bad staff management.

Recruitment and Training Cost Per Recruit   This indicates the resources spent on hiring and training staff and is useful in putting staffing policies into a financial perspective.

Payroll Administration Cost Per Person   This indicates the cost per person of processing the payroll. It is useful for comparison to similar costs from bureaux that provide an alternative service.

Sales and Marketing

Number of Customers; Ratio of One-Time Customers; Number of Customers Lost (By Reason); Number of Customers Gained (By Source)   Such statistics can be used to monitor selling workloads and the effect of marketing campaigns.

The above list is indicative only and in practice would need to be tailored to the industry and the particular circumstances of the business. However, it does serve to show that statistical measures and per-unit costs can be derived to help in cost control. Since the main aim must be to track whether cost reduction initiatives are biting, long-term trend analysis is relevant and graphs are an obvious method of presentation. Examples are shown in figures 12.3 to 12.6. It is still a case of looking at the scoreboard, but hopefully the scoreboard is more illuminating than a mere comparison of actual costs with a budget.

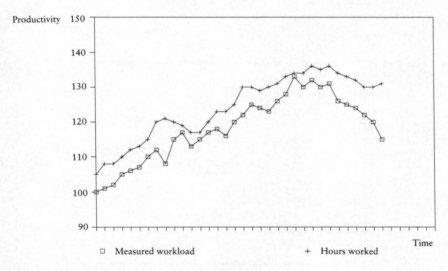

Figure 12.3   Productivity trend, previous 36 months

Comment: This graph shows we have major problems with the new product line. The level of retraining has been seriously underestimated and there is considerable down time to adjust equipment. Extra shifts are needed to restore production levels.

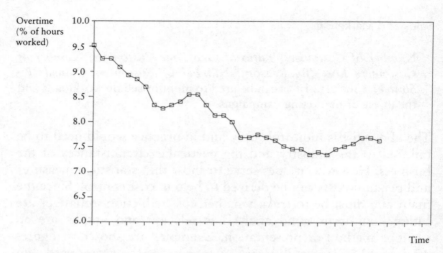

Figure 12.4   Overtime as a percentage of hours worked, previous 36 months

Comment: Recent increases in overtime are a result of the new equipment problems. Scope exists to increase overtime but a second shift would be more cost effective.

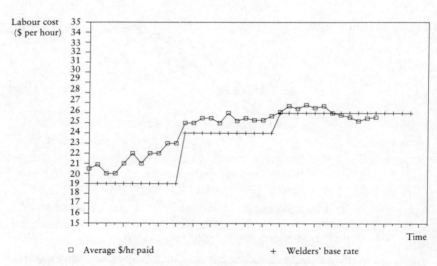

□   Average $/hr paid   +   Welders' base rate

Figure 12.5   Labour cost per hour, previous 36 months

Comment: Using the welders' wages as a comparison, it can be seen that the overall hourly cost has been contained by a shift towards unskilled labour. This trend will continue with the new automated equipment.

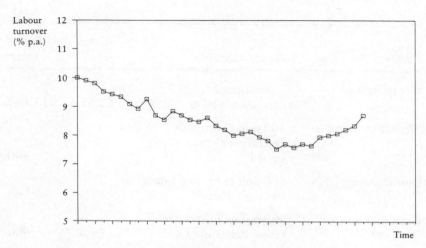

Figure 12.6   Labour turnover percentage per annum, previous 36 months

Comment: Labour turnover is still rising, imposing extra recruitment and training costs. This is mainly because of recruitment by the new car plant, which should slow down soon and cause turnover levels to decrease again. The improved health benefits scheme does not seem to have had any impact.

Comprehensive Measurement

> I would like to use a comprehensive system to rate the business performance of the managers. It must measure all the key factors that will make us a successful business.

Profit is usually too simplistic to be used as a comprehensive measurement method, with other targets being needed to measure other parts of the business process. Amalgamation of all these targets can be done by using a points score system. The points can then be added up and used to summarize total performance. The big advantage of this method is that the points can be weighted to reflect the relative importance of various factors. The example in figure 12.7 demonstrates the concept. The profit rating reflects a motivation to maximize profits, but it could be better expressed in terms of return on capital employed. New customers, lost customers, customer service and staff turnover reflect strategic issues within the company. The customer service rating could be measured by a periodic standard survey of customers. The audit rating might reflect a basic financial audit or a full operational audit.

Factor	Points available	Actual result	Points score
Contribution	1 point per $1,000 exceeding $1.2m	$2.85m	1,650
New customers	100 points for each key target client signed	3	300
Lost customers	500 points for loss rate less than 10%	12%	nil
Customer service	400 points for service rating better than 85%	89%	400
Staff turnover	500 points for staff turnover less than 35%	22%	500
Audit rating	−500 for unsatisfactory +100 for satisfactory +200 for very good	XXX	−500
Business ethics	−500 points for any legitimate complaint	none	nil
Total Points Score			2,350

Rating: 1,500 – 2,000 points   Satisfactory
2,001 – 2,500 points   Good
More than 2,500   Excellent

Figure 12.7   The Fine Measurement Corporation performance rating for the year ended 31/12/X6: Manager, North West Division

The business ethics rating is arguable but is a real issue in many organizations. In this example the company has ethics guidelines and a 'legitimate complaint' would be a breach of those guidelines. It could be that scoring ethics on a points basis is totally inappropriate because it is such a subjective issue. Furthermore, it could be construed as legitimizing a breach of guidelines, in that it only gives rise to a loss of points, when in fact the breach should be dealt with by censure, demotion or dismissal. None the less, it is included here for the sake of provoking debate.

Most of the statistical measures are effectively counted in the profit because if the statistics are optimized then so is the profit. The difference is that the statistical measures are related to strategic issues that may have long-term profit implications. Furthermore, they allow managers to consider themselves successful even if they have short-term profit problems.

Structuring the weighting is very much a trial and error exercise and should reflect the chief executive's rating of priorities. It can be specific to individual managers or uniform across similar types of business unit. The weighting could also be adjusted during the year to reflect changed priorities, but care needs to be taken not to discredit the system by 'moving the goal posts in the middle of the game'. A system of points scoring is most suited to a performance-based bonus system.

Comprehensive Audits

> I want to integrate the internal audit function into the control process. At present they seem to be only answerable to the external auditors.

Internal audit functions have evolved mainly as a mechanism for reducing charges from the external auditors. The theory is that the routine checking can be done in-house at much lower rates than those charged by the auditing firms. In some cases the internal audit function has been upgraded to conduct comprehensive audits which extend beyond the bookkeeping system and into day-to-day operational matters.

In most cases it is cheaper to run an internal audit department than to pay $80 an hour for a raw recruit in one of the big auditing firms, especially since that person will waste an inordinate amount of the client's time while being instructed on the difference between a debtors ledger and a creditors ledger. Apart from cost savings, an internal audit function is a useful training ground for accountants as it gives them a detailed view of the whole of the company.

Internal auditing can safely be taken one step further, to the job of ensuring that various corporate standards are being complied with: for example, that all the assets are properly insured, that personnel policies are observed and that key registers are up to date. This sort of checking may be mundane, but it provides a worthwhile service to the business as it is always the trivia that falls away first when work pressures build up.

Taking internal auditing to the next step, comprehensive audits, is unlikely to have any lasting success as comprehensive auditors have to be given a wide brief so that they can look at all facets of the operation. The auditors will have to justify their existence with a continual flow of criticism and comment. The manager under review is certain to attack any criticism most strenuously. Auditors will often only be able to rely on their own opinion, which is inadequate evidence when tackling a manager who sees his or her career progression threatened. The senior executives are placed in a difficult position: should they support the line manager or should they support the auditors? They cannot win either way.

If the auditing function adopts a consulting role, they may initially receive a few 'clients'. But most managers can think of more pleasant ways of spending their time than in receiving critical review, and eventually the queue of clients will dwindle to nothing. Effectively, comprehensive auditing is a vote of no confidence by the senior executives in their subordinates and in the normal control systems. As such it will not solve any problems and may cause some of its own.

13

Systems Development

This chapter looks at the accounting infrastructure needed to develop and support management control of the business. While most systems evolve gradually to match the fabric of the organization, every once in a while it becomes apparent that the evolution has moved away from perfection and a concentrated effort is needed to put the control system back on track.

Apart from the problem of unwelcome mutations during the evolution of the system, another practical aspect is that after a while most astute operators learn how to foil the system and defeat its control purpose. No control system can be beyond manipulation and the best that can be hoped for is that the tricks will take several years to become widely known. Then some of the holes in the system will need to be plugged. Inevitably this will open other avenues for the astute upwardly mobile executive.

So the business has to allow its control system to grow and change gradually to match the changes in operations and structure of the business. It also has to be ready to redraw the system periodically, to tighten it here, loosen it there, reject outdated theories on business management and perhaps critically accept more modern concepts.

Systems Design

I accept that we need to upgrade the management control systems and I know a smart young fellow in the Economics Research Department that should have a go at it.

The design of reporting systems is a specialized task requiring knowledge of accounting concepts and computer systems, combined with a detailed understanding of how the business is managed. When the reporting system starts working to full effect, it will have a major influence on the operation of the organization. It is not a task that should be delegated to a well-intentioned amateur.

The required attributes of a management reporting systems designer, or design team, are:

- time to research, design, test and market concepts and to train users: this means it is not practical for the designer simultaneously to perform a full-time line job while the project is in progress;
- industry experience to reflect the dynamics of the business and talk the same language as the line managers;
- accounting experience to ensure the system has financial integrity;
- computer systems experience to know what is feasible and at what cost: the experience needs to encompass both the company's existing databases and modern computing techniques.

It could be argued that the systems designer should have skills in organization design and organization behaviour. These attributes may be nice to have, but great care must be taken to ensure that a management information project does not become sidetracked into a critique of the organizational structure. Gratuitous advice on management shortcomings is a sure way to kill any management information project. The systems designer should reflect the system as it exists, not as it should be. If there are genuine organizational structure problems, these will become evident in the operation of the reporting system and then may be corrected.

Usually a team combining the various skills has to be assembled as it is difficult to find any one person with all the required skills. Not many organizations have high-quality personnel who can be spared from day-to-day operations for several months and so consultants and contractors become useful. Apart from workload considerations, the advantages of hired-in assistance are that there is a large pool to choose from, they do not remain on the payroll once the job is done and they can be replaced at short notice if not performing to the required standard. On the other hand, a lot of valuable company expertise can walk out the door with them at the end of the project.

When using consultants, it is possible for the project to be seen to belong to the consultant rather than the company's executives, and this can be exacerbated if the project is controversial for whatever reason. When this perception occurs, line managers do not give the project adequate support. To overcome this, the project must be seen to be managed by the company and not totally delegated to the consultant.

The development phase of a management reporting system needs to be separated from its operation once implemented. The attributes required of a development technician differ from those of a person suitable to operate the live system. Perhaps some of the designers will actually run the live system, but it is more likely that their development skills will be transferred to other development projects.

The implementation work needs to be set up as a separate project and controlled as such with a budget, timetable and specific deliverables. The system will be designed to match the senior executives' management style and so their input is vital. This input can be obtained through a project steering committee which will oversee the design and physical progress of the project. Typical membership of such a committee would be:

- the senior executive (or his/her representative), to approve the concepts of the system;
- a senior financial manager, to monitor the impact on the financial reporting systems;
- a senior data-processing manager, to monitor the impact on data-processing systems;
- one or more line managers to have a say in the system design and its impact on their operations.

Having set up the structure for the project, one of the first tasks is to document the organizational structure (using an organization chart) and managerial responsibilities (using job descriptions). In a fast-changing or recently restructured business, the job descriptions may be absent or inaccurate and will have to be updated before further progress can be made.

Another early task is to document all the existing reports to see which ones are redundant and which ones must be retained. Most likely, some of the management reports were designed in response to a long-forgotten *ad hoc* enquiry and have become a routine report because no one is brave enough or knowledgeable enough to stop the report.

The major factors affecting system design and operation were discussed in chapters 9 to 12, but there are two important considerations to be remembered. Firstly, businesses are constantly evolving and the reporting system will need to be updated constantly after the project team has done its original work. Secondly, there needs to be a bridge between a design that is conceptually correct and that which is feasible in the short term. In the long run we are all dead, and none more so than a management reporting team working to a five-year implementation schedule.

Budget Management

> Now the business is getting bigger and more diverse, I am becoming more sympathetic to the financial controller's demands to staff a specialist budget department. Before I give it the OK, I want to know what to expect of them.

Producing an effective budgetary control system requires considerable work and co-ordination as it must involve most line managers. A typical process for setting the budget would be:

- senior executive strategy meetings and documentation of strategies;
- preparation of operational plans by line managers;
- consolidation of financial plans (budgets) and review by senior executives;
- fine-tuning of the budgets, as required;
- further senior executive review and presentation to the board;
- confirmation to the line divisions that their budgets are approved.

In a large organization, the time span for this process may be three months and may involve dozens of line managers. Planning and controlling the budget process is a full-time job for one experienced person for six months of the year.

The major tools for planning the budget are a timetable and detailed instructions for head office and line division staff. The timetable should be derived from critical dates, especially board meeting dates, and worked backwards to define other timings. If senior executives are going to be absent during critical times in the process, then alternative managers will have to be nominated, or timings altered. The planning instructions do not need to be an accounting manual but should spell out:

- guidelines to be used on the economic or general business environment (exchange rates, economic growth rates, inflation, etc.);
- whether any standard forms are to be used and, if so, how they should be completed;
- the type of executive comment required to accompany the budget;
- product guidelines where appropriate;

- who are the key contact points for budget administration;
- whether there are any changes in accounting or reporting principles (e.g. changes in transfer pricing rules).

Management of the process then includes ensuring that timetables and instructions are complied with and that there is an element of quality control on the validity of the budget, although it can be politically dangerous for an administrative support person to criticize the plan of an experienced line manager.

Confidentiality

Good management information is a two-edged sword. Great for us and equally great for our competitors should they get hold of it.

A company's management reports, if they are any good, are a tempting target for competitors as they reveal the company's strategies, tactics, cost structure and organizational structure. They might also display the strengths and weaknesses of the current operation. They could also be a source of embarrassment if made available to public interest groups that are in dispute with the company. Even if the reports are fairly cryptic to the layman, their release would still be embarrassing for information-based industries where data security is a contentious issue. So security of management reports is an important issue that has to be balanced against the need to inform a wide range of interested parties within the company.

Companies usually distribute information on the basis of 'the need to know'. To some extent this is inevitable, not only from a security point of view, but also to limit the wastage of managerial time spent reading irrelevant reports. The problem is, who decides who needs to know? How do 'they' know that the employee relations manager does not need to see the production reports? Furthermore, information is a political weapon within an organization as access to information confers authority on the reader, and limited access to information limits authority.

This issue is becoming more topical as companies move to electronic databases of management information, which allow much wider access than paper reports. To some extent, those companies using a secure computer network for management information can have greater comfort than those distributing huge quantities of paper each month. On the other hand, when personal computer systems are involved, they pose a greater risk because the whole machine can be easily stolen, including the stored data.

Installing proper security is a job for a security expert, such as a data-processing auditor, and it has to be accorded a high priority before the disaster, not after it. Some risk is inevitable and it is a question of managing the risk rather than being able to avoid it completely.

Operational and Management Reports

> I would prefer the line managers to receive far fewer reports and to really act on those they do receive. At present we are sacrificing quality for quantity.

When considering the frequency of reporting, it is necessary to try and delineate between *management* reports and *operational* reports. Operational reports are those required for an operator to do his or her job, examples being:

- payroll reports, to ensure people have been paid the right amount;
- stock status reports, to identify items out of stock;
- debtors ledger reports, to identify those customers who have not yet paid their accounts.

Management reports are those designed to supervise or manage an operation, examples in a similar context being:

- labour cost summaries, to identify total labour costs compared to budget;
- stock holding summaries, to monitor stock turnover trends by major category of stock;
- a working capital report, which would include a summary of the average number of days of sales not yet paid for.

Operational reports are usually vital to effective day-to-day control of the function and therefore receive the highest priority. They have to be produced as frequently as the operator is supposed to do his or her job.

Management reports have a less immediate impact than operational reports as the time span for instituting corrective action is longer. Consequently, they are produced less frequently and, in the eyes of some systems programmers, receive a lower priority. The normal frequency for management reports is monthly, basically because accounting systems work around a monthly routine. This is satisfactory in most businesses, while some businesses need weekly management reports and others are satisfied with quarterly management reports.

Most good managers would view the management reports as a confirmation of what they already know, having sensed the status of the business through normal day-to-day interaction with operational personnel. Frequency of reporting depends on how quickly the underlying business can alter such that the manager needs to be made aware of the change. The effect of unexpected change varies greatly from one business to another, and within a business. Within a bank, branch managers may only need to see their branch reports quarterly, whereas the managers of foreign exchange dealers would want to see their results daily.

It is worth the effort of classifying reports into the categories of operational and management. Operational reports are essential and must receive the highest priority.

Exception Reporting

I remember many years ago when I was the maintenance engineer, I only received reports on problems. Why can't we apply this to the monthly management reports and so cut out a lot of wasted paper?

Exception reporting is heavily used in 'operational' systems, whereby the computer contains preset parameters and items are reported for action only if they are outside these parameters. Typical examples are:

- any debtors' balances older than forty-five days;
- any stock that has not moved for sixty days;
- any purchase order open after the due delivery date;
- any stock balance that is greater than ninety days' usage or less than ten days' usage.

The parameters can be varied by the application systems programmer to suit the context of the business. Exception reporting is vital in most large-scale computer systems as it saves the operators' time and focuses their attention on only the critical matters. If it can be used so extensively in operational systems, perhaps it has application in a management reporting system.

A senior manager with, say, ten managers reporting to her would receive numerous reports each month. In many cases there may be nothing in the reports warranting detailed attention, yet she still has to check all the reports to ensure she has not missed something important. At this point, there is a desire to try some form of reporting whereby only exceptional items are reported. Although it has the superficial attraction of reducing the senior manager's workload, the difficulty is in trying to define that which constitutes an exception. The possibilities for defining an exception are:

- variances to budget or last year, either in percentage terms or in absolute values;
- variances as a percentage of profit or total income or total sales.

The parameters could be unique to each business unit or uniform throughout the group. Setting the parameter in relation to the budget presumes the budget is a solid benchmark, which may not be the case. Exception reporting in comparison to an imprecise budget will show up many exceptions and hide some items that are coincidentally close to budget. Likewise, comparisons to last year presume there is a close continuity between one year and the next. Setting the parameters in relation to total sales, costs or profit does allow for ranking in some sort of priority.

Exception reporting is unlikely to save any underlying clerical effort because all the base reports still have to be prepared. The only thing it really would do is to cull the information before it progresses higher up the organization.

Apart from the difficulty of setting valid exception parameters, the major drawback of the use of exception reporting is that it promotes a scientific approach to business management which sidelines the intuitive aspects of management. In effect, the reporting system says 'we only need to know of something if the computer says we should know'. This is a dangerous precedent in that it confers far more reliance on the reporting system than is ever warranted.

The practical alternatives for senior executives who receive too many reports are:

- to reduce the volume of reports to, say, one page per division per month, with a full report each quarter;
- to have an experienced assistant go through the reports and highlight any issues that the senior executive should be aware of: the executive would then only address the highlighted matters;
- to pass the reporting decision to the line managers by saying to them 'only give me a detailed monthly report if you think it contains something I should be aware of'.

These solutions are more viable than placing reliance on programmed exception reports.

User Computing

> Whenever we want to make changes to the management reporting systems, the computer experts tell us that they have an eighteen-month backlog of work, and once they get round to the job it will be very costly. I thought all this new computer hardware and software that we have invested in meant we could speed up the whole development process.

While computers provide wonderful opportunities for processing data to facilitate management decision-making, they can also be a bottomless pit of frustration as the expectations fail to materialize. So the trick is to gain a feeling for what computers are able to provide, as against that which is just wishful thinking.

The major constraints in computing, from an accounting viewpoint, have been those of capturing the source data and then of obtaining the professional resources to massage the data into information. The source data are likely to remain a constraint as there will always be restrictions on the amount of keyboard entry that field staff should do just to satisfy obscure management information needs. The professional resources constraint is rapidly disappearing with the increased power of personal computers and easy-to-use software: this environment is termed *user computing*.

The mainframe computer has to be a rigid, tightly controlled and cost-effective environment. The investment in hardware and data is certain to be very significant. It has to run to strict deadlines to support field operations. It is unlikely to have much spare capacity as computer processing capacity tends to act like a vacuum with a large backlog of development jobs just waiting to fill up any gaps in the routine schedules. It is also likely to be short on skilled technicians, and those available are certain to want to give their priority to customer-oriented production jobs. Against this background, there is little scope for the semi-literate computer user to interrupt the normal schedules with management information jobs.

The answer to a lot of these constraints is to take the data off the mainframe computer in small manageable chunks and to process them on mini or micro computers. There are a number of computer products that make user computing a pragmatic and flexible approach, not only from the novice user's viewpoint, but also for the specialist technicians, who can then concentrate on the critical jobs while not obstructing the 'quest for knowledge'.

User computing is not cheap, as it requires modifications to mainframe computer procedures, extensive user training and the purchase of numerous personal computers. Furthermore, the novice users are certain to waste much of their initial efforts, which is just part of the cost of introducing new ways of doing things. Its benefit is in moving the system development bottleneck into the users' court so that they can set the priorities rather than be beholden to the mainframe programmers.

In setting up a user computing environment, the mainframe databases have to be configured to allow user access. This work will largely depend on the nature of the existing systems, but it could involve several man-months of effort, plus increased security, back-up procedures and disk storage. Then a hardware connection to the mini or micro computer is required, plus associated software. This will require several man-months of effort to install and test, and to train the users.

Having established the physical link to the mainframe, there needs to be a training and help facility so that the user does not need to bother the production technicians when things go wrong. This technical support facility may require one or two people full time.

At the user end, hardware and software is required which will range in cost from $3,000 for one micro computer to many times this price for a local area network which connects numerous personal computers. A trait of user computing is that novices become overnight 'experts' and attempt to influence hardware purchases. To some extent this is desirable in that additional machines can be purchased to meet specialist requirements, which the user is best able to define. On the other hand, without discipline and planning there will be a profusion of incompatible micro computers that will eventually cause inefficiency and wastage.

User computing is set as the future direction of computing for management information purposes. The software and hardware are readily available and there are no end of frustrated computer buffs just dying to play with the data. However, the annual improvements in price-performance of personal computer hardware are so dramatic that there is the temptation to hold back on investment until the latest model appears. Furthermore, these rapid developments destroy the resale value of used equipment, yet the computer buffs always demand the latest equipment. Strict cost justification of user computing and management information is an impossible exercise: any such investment is an 'act of faith' which can only be made by the business manager who needs the information to make decisions.

Data Definitions

I am sure there is 99% of the information we need on the computer systems already. The difficulty is finding out what is there, how accurate it is and how to get access to it. We must make full use of what we already have before collecting even more data, some of which is bound to duplicate what we already have.

User computing gives benefits in terms of speed of results and flexibility that are ideal for management information, but it is no substitute for routine customer support systems. When it comes to handling large volumes of customer transactions, large, tightly controlled mainframe systems are mandatory. The user computing function is not a realistic alternative to such systems.

User computing feeds off the mainframe databases and the needs for management information should be recognized when designing new systems. This does not mean that all the requests necessarily get programmed into the new system as some of the requests may be impractical. Management information specialists must ensure they are put on the list of people who have a say in the design of the new system. Once the mainframe system is up and running, it is too late to complain that it does not provide the required information.

To be able to make sensible requests of the mainframe systems designers, a reasonable computing knowledge is required. Asking for outlandish inclusions will no doubt mean that all requests will get heavily discounted, even the sensible ones. In the same vein, when the mainframe analyst says, 'This request is too hard', one needs sufficient experience to know whether to accept the proposition or to insist on the enhancement that had been originally requested. In making requests for more data, it is important to differentiate between that data which are computed automatically (e.g. average balance) and that which require additional data entry (e.g. age of customer). Extra work by field staff is something that has to be carefully considered and justified, whereas adding in a few extra programming routines should not be a major issue.

Tapping into the mainframe databases obviously means that there must be a clear understanding of the format and content of the files. Failure to understand clearly the nature of the data will lead to some monumental errors and wastage. The solution is a *data dictionary* which sets out exactly the details that are recorded in each field of the database. For example, the record that contains the 'customer balance' might be defined as:

Format: numerical with two decimal places
          positive signifies debit balance
          negative signifies credit balance
          currency indicator:
            D = dollar
            Y = yen
            L = pound, etc.
          age indicator:
            X = balance under 30 days
            Y = balance 30–60 days
            Z = balance over 60 days
Source: invoice processing – nightly
          cash receipt – on-line
          journals – on-line, etc.

Without knowing that some of the balances are designated in Japanese yen, there would be plenty of scope for mistakenly running computer reports that show that the Japanese customers have the largest amounts outstanding.

Usually the information for a data dictionary is hidden away in the systems specifications and is not readily available to anyone except the mainframe systems analyst. To prepare a data dictionary, the systems specifications have to be examined and the information recorded in a systematic, easy-to-access format. A properly indexed computer system is ideal for this purpose, whether on a personal computer or on the mainframe.

Software Tools

The data-processing manager keeps telling me that there is a large amount of wastage in the user computing environment. He says that most of the users don't know what they don't know: they are using the wrong software for the job in hand. I think we have to allow for a bit of initial wastage.

What novice users do on their own personal computer is their own business, but if they want to touch any mainframe data then strict rules and standards must be followed. Providing users have 'read only' access, it is reasonable for them to be able to run small enquiry jobs and to extract the results of these jobs on to the personal computer for more sophisticated processing. There are various mainframe query languages, such as SQL, and connectivity facilities that allow data extraction by an informed novice user. Setting up the infrastructure and the rules and standards is definitely a job for the mainframe specialist.

In the normal financial analysis role there are three basic pieces of personal computer software that will doubtless cater for 90% of all possible needs. By standardizing on these types of program and also standardizing on a particular product, businesses can be fairly sure their staff are using the best tools available and that training and support efforts are minimized.

Spreadsheet programs, such as Lotus 123, were the breakthrough that brought user computing into the business world. The systems are powerful yet easy to use, with some reasonable results available after only a few hours of self-tuition. A person would be considered an expert on the system after two months of continuous use.

A spreadsheet system puts all of the data into the personal computer main memory while it works on it. This means that it does not have to keep reading and writing data from disks and therefore that processing is extremely quick. While this is the big advantage of spreadsheets, it also limits their scope, in that spreadsheets are inappropriate for processing large volumes of data. For this type of work a database management system is required.

Database management systems, such as Ashton Tate's Dbase IV, are remarkably powerful tools for processing large files – large in a personal computing sense means a file containing, say, 2,000 to 20,000 records. The price of this power is increased complexity compared to a spreadsheet program, although there are attempts in most packages to allow the novice to produce some rudimentary results after several days of training.

These database management systems contain a programming language that allows an experienced programmer to set up complex systems that can then be handed over to the everyday user. To learn the programming language would need six months of experience with perhaps two years to master the language. The Dbase product is the most widely used of such systems and, although there are similar packages with slightly better features, the popularity of Dbase means that there are plenty of contract programmers available to write and support Dbase systems. Most Dbase programs are issued to the user in a compiled form, which means that the program will execute much more quickly and the user cannot go into the program and change formulae. This can be a failing with spreadsheets, which are usually uncompiled, where users think they know better than the program author, and ruin the spreadsheet with some inappropriate tinkering.

Database programs can offer some form of data encryption or password controls to preserve confidentiality. These are not as sophisticated as would apply on a mainframe system and can be unlocked by an expert. This is a pressing reason why sensitive customer information should be kept off personal computers.

Because Dbase is such a widespread language, many supplementary add-on features can be purchased to cope with paper reporting, graphics and communications. It is another reason to stick with the industry standard rather than explore a slightly more obscure, but perhaps cheaper or better featured programming system.

Dbase is not a language for the novice and the best and most cost-effective results will be achieved by hiring in an expert contractor. Contractors must fully document all their work before they leave, and they must leave behind the 'source code' for their programs: these are the program listings before they have been compiled.

Word-processing packages have increased dramatically in sophistication and now virtually allow the layman to engage in desktop publishing after several days of experience. This gives opportunities to provide routine management reports in a high-quality presentation. It is simple to link word processing, spreadsheets and database management systems, for example, so that the word processor produces letters using data held in the spreadsheet, or the spreadsheet uses data held in the database management system.

User Computing Example

User computing sounds as if it only moves the bottleneck from the computer centre to the accounting department. I need to see a real-life example.

The author has recently implemented a large-scale user computing system in Australia which is described here to demonstrate the benefits, pitfalls and costs of user computing. The system serves 100 users with monthly financial and statistical data extracted from the mainframe systems. All users have access to their own data on their own personal computer. The system replaced a mainframe paper reporting system that ran quarterly and required $2 million and five years to implement. The new system cost $250,000, took six months from design to implementation and offers a far higher degree of sophistication. It uses techniques that were hardly on the drawing board ten years ago when the original reporting system was being implemented. The new system has been in operation for one year without disaster, and there has been experience gained along the way which will be described to assist people undertaking similar projects.

System Outline

The system provides financial and statistical data dissected by geography, product and relationship manager. Twenty-four months of historical actual data are available, as well as remainder of year forecasts, current year budgets and next year budgets. These data are available through a menu-driven Clipper (compiled Dbase III Plus) program, with numerous failsafe features to protect the system from errors. Since it is entirely menu driven, it can be used by people with no computer experience. There are 100 interactive help screens in the system to explain the data to the user. The help screens can be refreshed each month so that the user is informed of any changes to the data definitions.

The system is primarily designed to be run at regional offices by the regional manager and his or her assistant. The branches (each region has up to thirty branches) do not have personal computers and so paper reports are printed in the regional office and distributed to each branch as the regional manager feels appropriate. Some regional managers issue paper reports on an exception basis, while others provide a whole suite of reports to each branch each month.

The main benefit of this system is that it allows multi-dimensional analysis of performance in any way that seems appropriate to the regional manager. For example, if the current focus is on pricing, then information can be viewed by product or by branch or by manager, against historical actuals or plans or remainder of year forecasts. Next month, the focus could be on the control of overtime, in which case a similar analysis of overtime is available. All data are available numerically, on screen or paper, or graphically. Each screen has about a three-second response time.

User Data

The volume of user data, 800 megabites, is far too large to be put all on one personal computer. Thus users only receive the data pertaining to the people who report to them individually, namely:

National manager:	national summary
	each state
State manager:	own state
	each region
Regional manager:	own region
	each branch
Branch manager:	own branch (paper reports only)

State managers also receive the national summary so they can compare their state against the other states.

Data are transmitted monthly via mainframe links to the state office, or directly to those regional offices that have mainframe connections. For regional offices without a mainframe connection, floppy disks are produced which the Dbase program automatically loads on to the hard disk after checking that the data belong to that region.

Each month, only the additional month's data are transferred and the personal computer gradually accumulates the historical data. When regions are restructured – that is, when branches are moved from one region to another – the whole history for both regions has to be refreshed to encompass the new structure and provide continuity of historical analysis. Numerous data files are required, plus files that contain the organization structure, product names and help screen data.

Personal Computer Programming

The personal computer program is written using Dbase III Plus compiled using Clipper. The program has 14,000 lines of code and occupies 320k of RAM, which has caused problems where users have been running memory-resident programs, such as Sidekick, causing the computer to crash from inadequate memory. This was rectified by using program overlays that limit the need for main memory space. In the first twelve months of operation, ten updates of the software have been available. The program contains its own testing system whereby it runs against standard data and produces control reports which identify possible programming bugs.

The response time is heavily dependent on hard disk access times, with most screens appearing in less than three seconds. Fragmented hard disks can increase this to twenty seconds and so a program to tidy up hard disks was instituted, with good effect. An initial problem was that all 100 users had to be using exactly the same version of the operating system, whereas prior to implementation there were numerous versions in use.

The personal computer program is renewed each month, unknown to the user. With each monthly data update, there is a file containing the new program, or the old program if there is no change. Once the old program has loaded the new program it deliberately stops the system, and when users restart the system they do so automatically using the new program. This has proved a very effective method of providing new features to the user without any technical intervention by the user. The users are reminded to go to the help screens to find out what the latest new feature has been.

User Interaction

The user mostly just has to press various menu options to obtain the data required or to change some of the system defaults, such as screen colour or disk drives.

The paper reports contain more detail than is available on the computer screen. Paper reports can be requested when looking at individual screens or as a batch job, in which various types of report can be specified for some or all of the branches. In a typical region, the monthly print job can take two hours, which is not excessive. However, it took six hours for one region with a badly fragmented hard disk.

Entry of budgets and estimates is done using specially designed input screens. The system produces a default budget or estimate based on certain assumptions that are programmed centrally. The user then goes in and changes the default result to match local peculiarities or expectations. The reasons for this tactic are twofold:

- sometimes the regional budget is done by a clerical assistant with no accounting skills, with the possibility of gross errors or omissions:

the default budget minimizes the chance of a major error being discovered late in the budgeting process;

- the system makes extensive use of bar graphs to display results and the user has the option of moving the bar graphs up and down, so changing the underlying data: this avoids the need for numbers to be keyed in by the non-accountant, who instead can just work from historical trends visually displayed. For this to work, there needs to be a default bar graph on the screen which can be juggled as necessary.

Once the budget or estimate is to the regional manager's satisfaction, the system produces a diskette that goes to the state office, where it is aggregated with the other regions to give a state total. This can then be further amended before being aggregated to give a national total.

Mainframe Processing

The system extracts data from numerous sources, but mainly from an MSA general ledger containing two million records which is heavily summarized before it reaches the user. The ready access to the data relies heavily on the corporate strategy of promoting user computing through the use of DB2. The data extraction from MSA DB2 is done using Focus programs containing 2,000 lines of code, plus numerous SQL utilities.

The MSA DB2 extract program is used to compress the data into a manageable form. For example, each branch has about 300 expenditure linecodes for various statutory, taxation and product management purposes. These are aggregated into about forty linecodes that are of relevance to a regional manager.

Non-financial systems used for sales and customer transactions are interrogated to give various statistics that are used to allocate income or to assist the regional manager. For instance, extensive data are extracted from a sales tracking system which records the volume of own products sold, as well as third-party products sold on an agency basis. It also captures the commissions earned from agency sales. The personnel system provides statistics on the number of full-time and part-time staff.

Data are moved between the mainframe and the PC using a standard piece of software called Netmaster PC which compresses the data and operates very effectively. Its main benefit is that it knows where to recommence if there is an interruption during the transmission. The software previously being used was much slower and the whole transmission had to be restarted if there was any interruption: very frustrating when it occurs after twenty-nine minutes of a thirty-minute job.

Implementation

The system was designed in concept over a period of two or three days, and a brief demonstration system was simultaneously written in Basic which incorporated the major features and dummy data. This provided sufficient specification for the mainframe and PC programmers to work in parallel knowing what they were supposed to achieve. The demonstration system was shown to users to gain their acceptance of the system concepts.

Within four months, fairly complete systems were demonstrated to the state divisions, which instituted training for the regional offices. Within six months, the system ran live and the old system of paper reporting was dismantled. All users initially received twenty-four months of historical data to allow trend analysis.

User training was minimal as it was felt that menu-driven design and the help screens would allow all users to train themselves. This proved to be successful; however, it took the users much longer to learn how to interpret the underlying information.

Without the user computing infrastructure, a similar project would have taken several man-years of mainframe COBOL programming, and therefore would not have been attempted. It was reliant on hiring two highly experienced and effective contract programmers: two good people being worth an army of less talented people.

User Reactions

The demand for management information is totally elastic. Nobody accepts that what they have is enough, and so there are still urgent requests for yet more data. In terms of cost effectiveness, the system described above has been successful as it has replaced many labour-intensive clerical exercises. However, it seems to have spawned a whole new industry of people looking through the data backwards, forwards and sideways trying to understand what is really happening to the business. Half of this effort may be worthwhile, the other half will no doubt be wasted. As with advertising, nobody knows which half of the effort is being wasted.

The following trade names have been used in this chapter: Lotus 123 is a registered trademark of Lotus Development Corporation; Dbase III Plus and Dbase IV are registered trademarks of Ashton Tate Corporation; Clipper is a registered name of Nantucket Corporation; Netmaster is a registered name of Software Developments Pty Ltd; MSA is a registered name of Management Science America Inc.

Glossary of Accounting Terminology

absorption costing   Archaic concept of ascribing indirect costs to products or activities.

accrual   Bookkeeping allowance for some future income or cost.

acquisition   Purchase of a company or fixed assets.

actual cost   Factual amount spent.

asset   Item that has some value to the business.

breakeven   Sales volume at which income equals costs.

budget   Financial representation of a target or constraint.

capital (equity)   Funding of the business that has been provided by the owners.

capital expenditure   Expenditure on fixed assets (e.g. the production machinery), cf. revenue expenditure.

cash flow   Difference between cash received and cash paid.

chart of accounts   List of codes, descriptions and rules used to record transactions in the general ledger.

contingency   Allowance for possible expenditures.

contingent liability   Amount that may have to be paid in the future, usually dependent on the outcome of legal action or a guarantee.

contribution   Difference between income and direct costs for a business segment.

cost   Amount of resources used, usually expressed in money terms.

cost behaviour   Understanding of the nexus between activity levels and cost levels, i.e. the determination of variable and fixed costs.

cost centre/profit centre/responsibility centre/management centre   Discrete activity or area of responsibility for which income and/or costs can be segregated.

cost of goods sold   Value of goods for which income has been recognized.

creditor   Person to whom the business owes money.

current asset   Asset that can be converted into cash in the normal course of business within the next, say, twelve months.

current liability   Liability that will have to be settled within the next twelve months.

debt   Amount owing to a creditor or lender.

debtor   Person who owes money to the business.

depreciation   Estimate of the reduction in value of an asset.

direct cost   Cost that is clearly traceable to an activity or product.

discounted cash flow (net present value and internal rate of return)
Financial analysis technique that recognizes that delays in paying or receiving money have a value in terms of the interest income forgone.

effectiveness   Measurement of whether a desired result has been achieved.

efficiency   Ratio of inputs to outputs.

equity   Extent to which the owners (or people who take a share of profits) have funded the business, in comparison to the funding provided by lenders.

estimate   Prediction of the future.

exceptional, extraordinary or abnormal item   Income or expenditure that is isolated from the normal reporting so as not to distort performance trends.

expected value   Future costs or income reduced by the probability of their occurrence.

expense   Use of resources.

external auditor   Representative of the stockholders who checks the quality of the statutory financial reports.

FIFO, LIFO, average cost and weighted average cost   Bookkeeping methods for deciding on inventory valuations and the cost of sales.

fixed asset   Asset held for long-term usage.

fixed cost   Cost that does not vary in proportion to the volume of activity that is under consideration.

flexible budget   *See* output budget.

forecast   Prediction of financial or operational causes or effects.

funds flow statement   Explanation of the movement of cash between two dates.

gearing (ratio)   Ratio of equity funding to debt funding.

general ledger   Official summary of all financial transactions.

goodwill   Difference between the price paid for a business and the value of assets recorded in the books of that business.

guarantee   Undertaking to ensure payment or performance.

hedge   A contract designed to avoid possible future losses on financial risks.

historical cost accounting   Conventional concept that all assets are recorded in the ledger at their original cost; the cost may subsequently be reduced (written down), on the grounds of prudence.

income   Value received.

income and expenditure account   *See* profit and loss account.

indirect cost   Any cost that is not a direct cost.

intangible asset   Asset that lacks physical substance.

interest   (1) Price of borrowing (or lending) money. (2) Part ownership of a company or project.

inventory   Stock of goods.

investment   Cash outlay.

job costing   Method of recording the costs for unique pieces of work.

labour on-cost   Cost that is additional to wages and that arises from the use of labour.

learning curve effect   Build-up of expertise through repetition of a task.

ledger   Any financial record.

limited liability (incorporation)   The separation of the legal existence of a company from the legal existence of its owners.

liquidation   Conversion of assets to cash.

long-term liability   Debts repayable more than twelve months hence.

management accounts   Financial reports used within a company, i.e. not for external consumption.

marginal cost or income   Cost or income caused by small increases in volume of an activity or product.

material   (1) Physical resource. (2) Accounting significance.

matrix management   Organizational structure whereby a person may simultaneously have two or more direct superiors.

merger   Euphemism for takeover.

mix   Composition of a basket of costs or products.

operating statement   Routine financial or statistical report.

operational plan   Statement of intended future physical activities.

opportunity cost   Income forgone by pursuing a course of action.

output budget   Method of establishing a budget where there is some measure of output or activity that can be related to costs.

overhead   *See* indirect cost.

payback period   Time taken to recoup the original investment.

prime cost   *See* direct cost.

process costing   Calculation of the cost of products that go through continuous manufacturing processes.

profit   Difference between income and costs.

profit and loss account   Statement of all income and costs.

project   (1) To make an estimate. (2) Separable piece of work with a start date and an end date.

provision   Bookkeeping allowance for future costs.

quarterly balance   Preparation of three-monthly statutory accounts.

quotation   (1) Selling price advised to the customer. (2) Admission to have shares traded on the stock exchange.

reserve   Archaic concept that records certain profits that should not be distributed to shareholders.

result(s)   Profit or profit statement.

return   (1) Form. (2) Management report. (3) Rejected sales or purchases. (4) Reward for investment.

revenue expenditure   Expenditure on raw materials and their conversion into a saleable product.

risk   (1) Interest rate risk: the risk that interest rates may vary. (2) Credit risk: the risk that a debtor may default. (3) Currency risk: the risk that exchange rates may move. (4) Liquidity risk: the risk of insufficient cash. (5) Operational risk: the risk of technological problems. (6) Market risk: the risk arising from competitors' actions. (7) Price risk: the risk that cost or income prices may vary.

Sales   Value, or volume, of goods or services passed to the customer.

segment   Subset of the market.

sensitivity analysis   Financial modelling to test the effect of alternative assumptions.

set-up cost   Cost of making ready for a new job.

shareholders' (stockholders') funds   The amount of balance sheet funds that have been put in by the investors, by way of either cash or retained earnings.

shares   Units of ownership of a company.

standard cost   Target or estimate of actual cost based on engineered performance standards.

stock   (1) Inventory. (2) Unit of ownership of a company.

sunk cost   Historical cost that is irrelevant to current decisions.

takeover   Acquisition of the majority voting rights in another business.

tax   Usually refers to taxes that are calculated as a percentage of profits.

transfer price   Price, or act, of selling goods or services from one department to another within the same firm.

underwrite   (1) To guarantee satisfactory performance by someone else, or the success of a project or financial deal. (2) To insure a risk.

valuation   Estimate of the cost or selling price of an asset.

variable cost   Cost that moves in correlation to a measurable level of activity.

variance   Difference between two amounts, usually actual and budget results.

variance analysis   Act of understanding the reason for variances.

write off   To reclassify an asset as an expense.

yield   (1) Ratio of inputs to outputs. (2) Ratio of profit to investment.

zero-based budgeting   Budgeting technique that requires annual re-justification of an activity and its costs.

Index

Decision *Accounting*

USING ACCOUNTING FOR MANAGERIAL DECISION-MAKING

GORDON FRASER

A manager faced with a wide ranging role must have a good grounding in the concepts of financial control. Immersion in the technical detail of accounting is unnecessary and effort has to be focused on using information tools to make decisions. The manager must be able to tailor the control systems to match the way he or she wants to manage the business.

This book clearly demonstrates how the manager can relate accounting information to the logic of the decision process, stripping away the technical jargon and historical conventions that normally bedevil accounting systems. It is not a book about techniques, the preserve of the professional accountant, but about understanding concepts and, as a consequence, knowing the right questions to ask.

The manager must demand relevant information from his accountant and the book clearly brings together these demands and the relevant concepts: *funding and cash flow control*; *profitability evaluations*; *capital investment*; *costing and pricing*; and *organizational control*. It will make managers more *effective* and consequently will be essential reading for the business manager, and also for the accountant trying to meet a manager's needs for clear financial information.